OUR FRACTURED IMAGE

The source of humanities' burdens and struggles

Richard A. Hindmarsh, MD

Fractured Resilience Publishing

ISBN 9798625539494

Library of Congress Catalog Number 2020905232

CONTENTS

Title Page

INTRODUCTION

We live in an age of abundance. We have a wealth of food, distractions, entertainment, possessions, and an overabundance of information. We have all we could need, but we still want more. With all we have, you would think we would also have an abundance of contentment. Instead, we have a wealth of discontentment. It does not matter if you have a lot or have just enough to survive; we all struggle with the same significant issues. Suicide and addiction rates are climbing as we continue to anguish amid our affluence. We struggle with factors that have been the cause of turmoil since the days of the first man, Adam. So, you may be wealthy, or you may be impoverished, you may be famous, or you may feel insignificant. Your status does not matter; we all struggle with the same issues. We all wrestle with the pain of feeling isolated and alone. We all struggle with our meaning and purpose. We are all crushed by an awareness of our weakness and how powerless we are where it matters. We all walk under the dark cloud of our mortality as we work hard to deny our eventual demise.

We struggle under the weight of emptiness with a felt distance between ourselves and our creator. These are the burdens we all share. These burdens cause unbearable pain and cry out for relief. We now live our lives focused on personal comfort at any cost. We become self-centered and self-protective. Our actions only increase our awareness of our isolation, meaninglessness, powerlessness, frailty, and emptiness. So, we push and strive even harder. We treat obstacles as offenses and become bitter in our relentless striving for comfort. As we reach out for support, what we get in return is misery. This overwhelming misery is experienced emotionally and physically and does not have a successful psychological or medical cure. So, what is the answer to this plague of despair?

When God created Adam, He placed him in a world He defined as being very good. With the breath of God, Adam awoke with a body and a spirit. Adam was different from the rest of the animals. Adam possessed the image of God. Somewhere in the intricate sequencing of humanities' DNA is the original God-breathed image. This image has the capacity for intimate, meaningful relationships with God and fellow man. This image was made for beneficial work that has meaning and purpose.

Work that would be fulfilling. The image also has a capacity for creativity and power. It can accomplish a plan with a purpose. This image was made to be immortal with the full awareness and appreciation of eternity. The understanding of death was not part of this image. This image also fostered a thorough knowledge that man was more than a physical being. Man was also a spiritual being, and within that spiritual part is where access to contentment existed. Adam was complete, as God intended, his body and his spirit were alive and well. But, like all men since, Adam wanted more. He turned his back on God and, in the process, opened the door for humanity's ongoing struggles. Since that time, man has been living with a fractured image. The image was to be our glory but has become the source of our anguish.

In our anguish and turmoil, there is some good news. God has provided a path of reconciliation so we can live today as God originally intended. We do not have to remain stuck in the mud of relentless misery.

CHAPTER 1 - NO TEMPTATION

"**N**o temptation [regardless of its source] has overtaken or enticed you that is not common to human experience [nor is any temptation unusual or beyond human resistance], but God is faithful [to His word - He is compassionate and trustworthy], and He will not let you be tempted beyond your ability [to resist], but along with the temptation He [has in the past and is now and] will [always] provide the way out as well, so that you will be able to endure it [without yielding, and will overcome temptation with joy]." 1 Corinthians 10:13 (AMP)

We are all enticed by the same temptation, especially at times of discomfort. The temptation is to turn our backs on God and pursue self-attainable comfort. Unfortunately, contentment pursued is never satisfied; it results in intensified efforts to achieve satisfaction at any cost. The definition of addiction is "ritualistic, compulsive comfort-seeking." What we desire is contentment, but contentment and comfort are two different things. Comfort only satisfies briefly, where contentment lasts a lifetime. You must pursue comfort, where contentment comes with the absence of pursuit. Comfort costs, contentment pays back. We desire contentment but want to remain in control, so we seek comfort, thinking it is contentment, and eventually, all we end up with is discontentment.

Life consists of a variety of experiences. Some of these experiences are positive, and some are negative. Some cause pleasure, while others cause pain. We face trials, temptations, traumas, burdens, and injustices. These various experiences make us feel unique as if no one else shares in the troubles I have had to face in my life. Our pain consumes our lives, and we are oblivious to the pain in others. Although our problems may appear to be different, the temptation to separate ourselves from God to seek other means to soothe our discomfort is the same. We are all equally tempted to murmur and find comfort on our terms. Our temptation is to partake in the sin of discontentment.

We have the example of the children of Israel coming out of Egypt in the first part of 1 Corinthians 10 and the book of Exodus. They suffered in misery as slaves for over 400 years. God sent them Moses, but they wanted more. They saw miracles performed at the hand of Moses, but they wanted more. They survived the plagues, but they wanted more. They painted the blood on their doorposts and saw their children saved, but they wanted more. They experienced freedom from slavery, but they wanted more. They saw the Red Sea part, and they walked across on dry land, but they wanted more. They saw Pharaoh's army defeated, but they wanted more. They were fed daily by food that fell from heaven, but they wanted more. They drank water from a rock that followed them as they journeyed, but they wanted more. They wandered in the desert for forty years, and their clothes did not wear out, but they wanted more. They followed a pillar of fire and a cloud, but they wanted more. They heard the audible voice of God, but they wanted more. They saw Moses carry the tablets written by the finger of God, but they wanted more. They saw Moses shine with the glory of God, but they wanted more. They wandered for forty years and died in the wilderness because of their sin, the sin of discontent. We have even a greater witness, but we still want more. We have God's holy scriptures, but we still want more. We have a historical record of prophecies fulfilled, but we still want more. We have the authentic witness of Christ, but we still want more. We have the history of Christ's death and resurrection, but we still want more. We have the recorded reports of those who witnessed Christ's death and resurrection, but we still want more. We have examples of thousands of godly men and women who have gone before us, but we still want more. We have the daily, moment-by-moment witness of the Holy Spirit, but we still want more. We have the example of the children of Israel who died in the wilderness because they wanted more, and we still want more. The children of Israel compared their situation to what they had experienced in the past, and they wanted more. Their sin of discontent caused them to die in the wilderness. Dissatisfaction today is the same as discontent in the day of Moses. It is a sin; it is turning your back on God; it is demanding God serve you, as opposed to you serving God. Discontent in the day of Moses left the children of Israel floundering in the wilderness, just like discontent today is causing Christians to flounder in their faith and miss what has been provided by a loving and gracious God. The discomfort leading to comparison will result in discontent. Discontent is turning your back on God and denying what Christ accomplished on the cross. Discontentment will destroy you; it will deafen your ear to the voice of the Spirit; it will weaken your faith; it will leave you discouraged and lead to all sorts of self-destructive behaviors.

So, how do we unravel this mess? What does it mean to live a contented life? What do we do with discontent? What are the discomforts we face in life that are most likely to lead to dissatisfaction?

The purpose of this book is to examine some of the significant causes of discomforts, propelling us in a self-destructive direction resulting in discontent.

We experience discomfort as being physical, emotional, relational, social, existential, or spiritual. Spiritual distress is a result of being separated from God. Existential unease is the philosopher's description of experiencing separation from God. This spiritual/existential discomfort is what eventually causes emotional, relational, and social distress. At times it may even be the leading force causing physical pain. These spiritual/existential elements of discomfort are deep and troubling. They affect all of us and every aspect of our lives.

The experience of ongoing discomfort leads to comparison. We compare how things used to be when we were younger and more energetic. We compare our situation to how things appear to be for others and their life experiences. This comparison leads to coveting, jealousy, and envy. We compare our present state to how we expect things should be and not to how they are. We also compare our experience to what messages we get from our world as to how things should be. We can also compare our present discomfort to what we believe God should be doing for us. If you find yourself doing this thought-dance of comparison, you need to be aware that you are living in discontent.

So, our felt discomfort, combined with constant comparing results in either discontentment, arrogance, or addiction. If it goes on long enough, it will always result in discontentment. If we can feel like we have succeeded, even briefly in gaining control of our comfort, it will result in arrogance. If we end up in the relentless pursuit of pleasure, it will end with addiction. It would be much better to start with the elements of discomfort and learn to deal with them more directly and productively. We will not be able to escape trouble, but the discomfort does not have to result in discontent. Peace and contentment are possible if we handle pain and discomfort God's way.

These sources of discomfort have been the subject of theologians and philosophers for centuries. As a group, they have been called the existential realities – the major everyday stressors all humans face. They are the burden of felt isolation, the struggle with meaning and purpose, the anguish of free choice and responsibility, the dread caused by the burden of mortality, and the burden of spiritual emptiness.

As stated in 1 Corinthians 10:13 (KJV), *"No temptation has taken you that is not common to man."* There is no hierarchy of troubling life experiences. Life experiences do not have the power to damage a human beyond repair, and no quality parenting or upbringing can prevent temptation. Adverse childhood experiences are terrible and should not occur, but if they do, it does not mean you have to remain broken for life – there is real hope.

Even if you have had a great upbringing, you are not immune to life's problems. You, too, will face the same temptations as everyone else, you will be tempted to turn your back on God and seek your way.

Do not forget: *"along with the temptation He [has in the past and is now and] will [always] provide the way out as well, so that you will be able to endure it."*

CHAPTER 2 - EXISTENTIAL BURDENS

Henry David Thoreau said: "The mass of men lead lives of quiet desperation and die with their song still inside them." Is that how you would like to live your life? A life of despair where you bury your potential, or would you like to live your life with creativity and enthusiasm? We have this overbearing weight in our chest, that communicates that something fundamental is not right. This weight has the power to hobble us and prevent personal growth. This weight is experienced as intense boredom, the awful pain of loss or failure, the tension of irresolvable conflict, the anguish of inadequacy, the oppressive darkness of aloneness, the despair of hopelessness, the restlessness of meaninglessness, and the angst of perpetual uncertainty. The source of this angst are the existential burdens.

These burdens are existential in that they are present in all humans; they are realities that are part of our essence. They are burdens in that they are a load we must carry, no matter how oppressive or worrisome. No one else can take these burdens for you. Every moment of our lives is pregnant with the potential for an existential crisis. A moment when we become paralyzed by questions regarding our life: does our life have any meaning, purpose, or value. We are at some level deep within our being aware of this potential and the impact it could have. We do our best to keep a lid on this angst through distractions, actions, denial, and superstitions. We live in an age ripe with the potential for an existential crisis, where the man of quiet desperation is not so quiet anymore.

If we are to have any hope of living a full and meaningful life, we need to address the following existential issues: the burden of isolation, the burden of meaninglessness, the burden of responsibility, the burden of mortality, and the weight of spiritual emptiness. If we do not address these areas, we will be ensuring our place as one of the people Thoreau describes as living a life of quiet desperation. Yes, we may have fleeting moments of delight, but are more likely to have seasons of despair as our distractions show themselves to be inadequate.

These existential burdens are a powerful force. If left unaddressed, they can lead to despair, greed, bitterness, anger, depleted resilience, and lost potential. If, on the other hand, you acknowledge these areas, and they are accepted and appropriately addressed, they can be a source of unbelievable energy, creativity, and spiritual awakening.

If we desire to be the vibrant, creative humans that God intended, then we need a plan for dealing with these profoundly troubling issues.

In Psalms 39:6 (TPT), we read: *"We live our lives like those living in shadows. All our activities and energies are spent on things that pass away. We gather, we hoard, we cling to our things, only to leave them all behind for who knows who."*

Do you feel you are living in a shadow? Do you think that your life has passed? You work hard, consider others, act justly, are compassionate, and empathetic – yet it is all for what? You still feel alone and useless, with no apparent purpose.

We are all aware of this potential for an existential crisis and the impact it could have. Instead, we do our best to keep it caged and live our busy lives disconnected from each other, confused about our purpose and abandoning our potential, feeding our desires, and starving our soul.

So, what are these overwhelming burdens that affect all men?

Firstly, is the burden of isolation. Isolation and the reality that even though we live in a world of many others, we often feel, and are, very isolated and alone. You can experience isolation at different levels. There is interpersonal isolation – where you feel physically isolated from others. You can also experience isolation as intrapersonal isolation, where in the presence of even loving, positive relationships there are areas where secrets exist, and there is a felt distance in the relationship. There is also existential isolation where it is not possible ever to experience the subjectivity of another human being. In other words, nobody knows me, and I don't really know anyone else. We live with a fear of rejection. We need to be aware of this reality, be willing to explore its significance, and accept it for what it is. It is also important to realize everyone else experiences this same sense of isolation. We live in a crowd of isolated individuals.

Another existential issue we struggle with is meaninglessness. Searching for meaning is a reality of human life. What it boils down to is the question, "why are we here, or why do we exist?" We can pursue meaning on three levels. We can seek false meaning, transitory meaning, or ultimate meaning.

False meaning is a type of meaning or purpose that is often just a pleasant, or unpleasant, diversion. It is the pursuit of activities for immediate pleasure that often are harmful. In the long run, the pursuit of food, drink, drugs, money, power, or any other action considered immediately pleasurable is not connected to any form of lasting meaning. These pursuits can be a useful diversion from the angst of these existential burdens for a season, but they will eventually be inadequate if they don't kill you first.

Transitory meaning is where the pursuit is not destructive, but neither does it give any lasting meaning or purpose. Developing skills, achieving success, receiving education, pursuing healthy interests, may not cause harm: they do keep us busy and distracted but do not provide any ultimate or lasting meaning.

We find ultimate meaning through a relationship with something or someone greater than us. This ultimate meaning transcends the other issues of relationship, mortality, and choice and can put those other areas into a proper perspective. The question is: how do you find this meaning?

The burden of free choice is another existential reality. We are in the privileged and yet, the terrifying position of being able to create who we are through the choices we make. The frightening part is that it is our personal and individual responsibility to make those choices. If you abandon your responsibility through living as a victim, with bitterness, fear, or anger, you are also giving up your power and ability to create a new you. It is ultimately your choice, a choice that should be a freedom and not a hindrance.

Another existential reality is the burden of mortality. Our eventual death is an issue all human beings face. For many people, the subconscious anxiety caused by a fear of death is behind a lot of their daily anguish. This fear is a reality we need to acknowledge and accept. It is not healthy to live oblivious to death or to live in constant fear of death. If you value and count your days, you are more likely to use them wisely.

Lastly, is the burden of spiritual emptiness; a self-centered life, disconnected from God and the universe.

Wrestling with how we fit in this complex universe is a significant burden. We, as individuals, are our only experience of the world, and that experience is very inadequate. God's creation is a complex entity of which we are only a small part. No matter how much we study and investigate, much of it remains a mystery. How we fit into this grand design is a cause for anguish. We know there is a designer, and we know we are not that designer. How should we relate to the designer?

These existential realities can either hold us in a pit of despair or direct us to a well of creative energy.

Let's take a little closer look at the impact of these existential burdens.

Back to Henry David Thoreau's quote, "The mass of men lead lives of quiet desperation." Unresolved issues with the existential burdens cause an undercurrent of unrest. This unrest is painful boredom that is unsettling, troubling, and at times feels like insanity.

Even though we may not be able to identify it, we know something is wrong, and we need to do something, anything, to lessen the pain.

This unrest drains our resilience, energy, vitality, and drive. It becomes a distraction from moving ahead with life. We are left carrying a heavy burden, and we are left drained and discouraged. We abandon our creativity and potential as we must use all our resources to carry the weight.

The discomfort caused by these existential burdens demands a solution, some level of comfort that will allow us to continue living our lives and not remain stuck in an existential crisis. We are willing to gain this comfort with little regard for the cost – our motto becomes "comfort at any cost." We are eager to spend whatever we must in the passionate pursuit of comfort through distractions like drugs, alcohol, hobbies, sports, entertainment, relationships, or work. But this feverish pursuit never brings us any substantial or lasting comfort. The relentless pursuit of pleasure leads to disaster. We are left drained, disappointed, and in despair.

The anguish caused by this life of quiet desperation can be consuming. It leaves us with no resilience and no desire to move ahead with our lives. At this point, we have lost our creativity, and options for our future seem nonexistent. It is no wonder people in this state, bury themselves in drugs, alcohol, or self-destructive activities.

It is not a big step from consuming anguish to terminal despair – a life of depression, chronic anxiety, psychosis, or suicide.

These issues are part of all our lives; they are part of what it means to be human.

Most often, these burdens take us on a path of slow destruction. But as we shall see, if handled productively, God's way, can have the power to transform us and awaken our creativity and potential.

I invite you to join me on this challenging journey to explore these burdens and see if we can find that path of freedom and potential - the way leading us back to God and the restoration of our God-image.

CHAPTER 3 - NO CONTENTMENT WITHOUT THE CROSS

L ife is hard, confusing, troubling, and at times, feels impossible. We all struggle with the burden and pain of isolation, meaninglessness, responsibility, mortality, and spiritual emptiness. Our goal during these times of difficulty is not complacency or comfort; our goal is contentment. A life free from discomfort would lack the challenges needed to grow. Yes, we have times when we would like to see things work out smoothly. We long for our environment to change to accommodate to our wishes, but what we desire is to know amid very troubling circumstances that we are still at peace and not destroyed emotionally.

Remember, *"no temptation has taken you, that is not common to man."* The significant struggles we face are the same. We all struggle with the pain of isolation. We feel we are alone, and no one understands us, and we do not understand anyone else.

We all struggle with finding our meaning and purpose. We know we are unique, but it can be challenging to discover what our mission is or even if we have a purpose, and at times, life seems meaningless. We all struggle with the fact we have free choice, and our decisions are our responsibility. These choices can seem to be freedom but also come with the consequences of guilt, shame, and remorse. We all struggle with our mortality, which in turn fosters denial and avoidance. Our time on earth is brief, and that thought is very troubling. All we currently know will be gone. We struggle with spiritual emptiness, the void within us when we stubbornly try to work out life in our power with our plan, under our control. At times it does not seem possible to trust God. We strive with all we must to serve ourselves, to achieve some level of comfort, and as we do our condition deteriorates, and our discontent grows.

So, we all struggle with the same major issues, yet we seem to think we are the only ones struggling. You may feel isolated, but you are not alone in that struggle. We are all tempted to turn our backs on God in similar ways, but don't forget the next part of the verse that He has provided a means of escape. God provided the way of escape through the work Christ accomplished on the cross. The focus of this chapter is to consider what Christ accomplished at the cross. We will also look at how this applies to our daily struggles. What does it mean that His yoke is easy, and His burden is light? At times life seems more of a duty and heavy responsibility than a blessing.

Most often, our discomfort and discontent do not lead us to the cross; it leads us to actions within our power and control. We strive to overcome uneasiness through denial, distraction, reaction, and minimization. All these methods seem to work briefly, but given time, they leave us more discouraged and emptier.

To control our discontentment and felt pain, we alter painful reality through denial. We deny we have a problem, or we minimize the seriousness of the problem. We deny our faults, and by pretending they don't exist, believe we will be able to hide our flaws. We deny our intent, pretending our intent or motives are pure and positive when they are self-protective. We deny our self-centeredness and selfishness, convinced our actions are to serve others. We use fantasy and superstition to strengthen our denial, removing our felt pain further from experience and reality. We can even use perpetual turmoil as a means of denial, believing that if my life is in constant upheaval, I have an excuse, and do not have to deal with the more significant realities and issues of life. Through a lack of gratitude, we can even deny the many blessings in our life. If I chose to live in denial as a means of controlling felt pain, then thanksgiving and gratitude will not be a part of my life. Gratitude dissolves denial, so if I am grateful, I would have to face the realities of life.

If denying is not our first choice of controlling discontentment, then we will often choose distraction. Distraction is a mild form of denial and can be an effective way of dealing with discontentment and pain. If you want to lessen the pain of a childhood immunization, distract the child with a noisy toy. We distract ourselves in many ways. We distract through entertainment. Movies, television, sports, computer games are all readily available and effective forms of distraction. Work can serve as a distraction, a way of avoiding dealing with or recognizing discontent in other areas of life. We can be distracted through education or additional learning. Self-help books are plentiful and can even offer some superficial benefit, but they can also be a form of ongoing distraction from the realities of life. We can be distracted by hobbies. We can be distracted fighting for a cause or being part of a group of like-minded people. It is not that any of these things can be called evil, they may be a valuable part of our life, but not if their sole purpose is a distraction. You still need to spend time addressing reality. We can achieve avoidance-distraction with ritual, the practice of a set of actions or procedures with an expected outcome. If I do things in a specific prescribed way, then God is obligated to bless me. If left uncontrolled, rituals can become compulsions, and compulsions can become obsessions, and the purpose of the action is wholly lost.

If distraction becomes ineffective, it is possible to take it another level and seek to numb ourselves effectively. It is possible for you to numb discontentment for some time with food, drugs, alcohol, gambling, sex, or commuter games. It is the comfort provided by these activities that make an addiction an addiction. Be careful; it is easy to go from distraction to addiction without even realizing it.

Another mechanism of dealing with discontentment is through reaction. Anger can be an effective form of self-protection when you feel threatened. Living as a victim and avoiding responsibility through blame and bitterness can feel like a safe place to hide from life's discontentment. Feeling special because of your unique situation or life-pain can be used to justify rebellion and even criminal activity.

We long for contentment. Denial, distraction, addiction, and overt reaction do not bring us more pleasure. These activities may be an effective means of avoidance, but in the long run, leave us with more discontentment.

What is contentment? If you ask, you will get many different answers. Most people would answer that contentment is the solution to an immediate life problem. Discontented people, from the beginning of time, have turned to their spiritual leaders; monks, shaman, mystics, rabbis, imams, priests, and pastors for the key to living a contented life. We also turn to our psychologists, philosophers, sociologists, and medical doctors to find the path to contentment. If all else fails, we can minimize your discontentment with a medication. We are even promised contentment by the advertising industry, which promotes their products as a cure for discontentment. Peddlers of counterfeit contentment fill our world. If a wave of contentment suddenly hit our nation, the jobless rate would skyrocket. Discontentment is good for the economy but cruel to the citizens. Contentment masquerades as many things, so to get a better handle on contentment, we need to evaluate what it is not.

Contentment is a vital part of healthy, productive living, but it is not a quality you can, through your self-generated efforts, achieve. Contentment is not a minimizing of expectations and learning to live in the moment. This minimization is just a combination of denial and complacency.

Contentment is not financial security. If you have enough finances for your basic needs, the rest or abundance does not add to your level of contentment.

Contentment has nothing to do with leisure time. Leisure as a sole focus of attainable peace will disappoint.

Contentment is not a physical state. You cannot obtain peace with an exercise program or diet. Good health is desirable, but it is not contentment.

So, what then is contentment?

Hebrews chapter 4 describes the contentment available to all children of God. It is the faith-rest that should be a part of every believer's life. Unfortunately, what we witness most often, or experience in our own lives, is a life where we believe in God, but faith-rest is lacking. Where is this promised land of rest? We seem to be willing to remain content our belief will get us to heaven while we continue to struggle with life's burdens. We are no different than the children of Israel; we believe in the promise but walk in the wilderness. Hebrews chapter four encourages us to walk in this faith-rest provided by God, "today." We do not have to be weighed down by the burdens of this life if we live by faith. We do not have to be imprisoned by the crushing aloneness of isolation. We do not have to be trapped or confused by meaninglessness, pressured by free choice and responsibility, or hobbled by the heaviness of our mortality or the emptiness of our spirituality.

"For those of us who believe, faith activates the promise, and we experience the realm of confident rest!" Hebrews 4:3 (TPT)

God has promised us His rest; this rest is real contentment. It is the freedom to be the authentic you. It is not a life of complacency. It is the ability to know God's plan for you and the ability to live that plan with passion and commitment. It is living with the belief and faith that God's rest and peace are more significant than any of the world's burdens or problems. God is our source, God is our provider, and we should be living free in service to Him.

"As we enter into God's faith-rest life, we cease from our works, just as God celebrates his finished works and rests in them." Hebrews 4:10 (TPT)

We cannot gain God's faith-rest by our works; it is provided, as a gift, bought with a price. Real contentment is only available through and because of the cross. The cost was high and He paid the price. Contentment seems to be out of reach because it is out of our reach; it is only available through the cross. All other forms of felt contentment are a minimization of genuine contentment. The only valid contentment is the faith-rest Christ died to purchase for us. For this reason, the burdens of life seem to escape resolution. They have no adequate resolution without the cross, but with the cross, there is a resolution, restoration, and rest. Hebrews 4:11 tells us this is not the "let go and let God" kind of complacent rest; we obtain this rest through diligence and effort. We need to allow God to search our hearts; we need to root out unbelief and ask God for faith. We need to seek Him with all our heart and not just seek Him enough to feel a little better about ourselves today. We also need to gain a growing appreciation for what Christ accomplished on the cross.

"So then we must give our all and be eager to experience this faith-rest life so that no one falls short by following the same pattern of doubt and unbelief." Hebrews 4:11 (TPT)

The children of Israel were able to visualize their lives in the promised land but did not have the faith to enter that land. We, too, should be able to imagine what life would look like if we lived in this faith-rest promise. Do we want to be like the children of Israel and miss the promise?

What would our experience of the burdens of life look like if we were to live by faith and experience God provided "faith-rest"?

Firstly, we would not see the burdens as burdens but as a vital part of the image of God alive in each of us. Our discontent comes from not living our lives in the image of God, as God intended. The image has not changed, but our relationship with God has changed. Contentment comes with "living the image." At the cross, Christ provided a way back to God, so we should now be able to live in His image as was initially intended.

"And by the blood of his cross, everything in heaven and earth is brought back to himself - back to its original intent, restored to inno-

cence again! Even though you were once distant from him, living in the shadows of your evil thoughts and actions, he reconnected you back to himself. He released his supernatural peace to you through the sacrifice of his own body as the sin-payment on your behalf so that you would dwell in his presence. And now there is nothing between you and Father God, for he sees you as holy, flawless, and restored," Colossians 1:20-22 (TPT) These three verses appear several more times in this book. Do not skip over them. They provide the answer to your life struggles. We need to live with a growing awareness of what Christ accomplished for each of us on the cross.

The image of God in us is fractured, but because of the work Christ accomplished on the cross, we can now renew our relationship with God and live the image and the life that He intended.

So, let's take a more detailed look at the burdens we all carry and then evaluate them with the knowledge of being made in God's image. Don't forget; there is restoration for our God-image through what Christ accomplished on the cross.

CHAPTER 4 - BURDEN OF ISOLATION

In Psalms 39:6 (TPT), we read: "We live our lives like those living in shadows. All our activities and energies are spent for things that pass away. We gather, we hoard, we cling to our things, only to leave them all behind for who knows who."

Do you feel like you are living in a shadow and lack substance? Do you think no one cares about you? So, what is this burden of isolation? How do we recognize it? How do we accept it, and how do we live, so we are not consumed by it?

The first step in learning how to deal with this existential burden of isolation is to acknowledge it exists and that it is a problem. Isolation is a deep, painful craving for connection. God created us with a longing for belonging. A longing that is never fully met. We experience isolation at different levels: we can experience it as interpersonal isolation – where we feel physically isolated from others and disconnected from the world.

We can also experience it as intrapersonal isolation where even in the presence of loving, positive relationships there are areas where secrets exist, and we feel there is distance in the relationship and no meaningful connection. There is also existential isolation where it is not possible to ever experience the subjectivity of another human being. It feels like there is no way I will ever be meaningfully connected. In other words, nobody knows me, and I don't substantially know anyone else. We live with a fear that if identified for who we are, others will reject us. We are afraid of being authentic.

We live in an age of accessible communication but a growing sense of isolation and disconnectedness. We seem to crave and demand connection more than ever. We search for and, at times, require relationships that will lessen the pain of loneliness. We also demand that these relationships validate our qualities so we might feel complete, achieve some sense of immortality, and confirm our life choices. We also request that these relationships confirm that our directions are worthwhile and that we are somehow spiritually intact and connected. Our current cultural connections have very little to do with who we are and more to do with how we present ourselves. We superficially join around shared beliefs, political affiliations, sports teams, gangs, and genres of music. We take less time to pause as a community to consider life and how we should live our lives.

We attend church less frequently. We have fewer funerals. We have fewer small group discussions about how to live and more superficial discussions around the latest computer games, cars, or sports teams. We have more superficial connections, but less meaningful relationships, and we are more willing to compromise or abandon our beliefs to feel like we belong. The community, my grandparents grew up in, needed each other; they would not have survived without the support of their family and neighbors. They worshiped together, they prayed together, and they spent time together. They did not go to sporting events or political rallies. They cried together at funerals and rejoiced together with the birth of a new family member. They were able to identify with a community, a community they needed, and a community that needed them. Unfortunately, we no longer need each other the way they needed each other. Our desire for connection has not changed in the last 100 years, but our need for each other has vanished. Our affluence has brought us many advantages, but it has cost us the value of a connected community.

The erosion of connectedness has also significantly impacted our interpersonal relationships. We may have more interpersonal relationships, but they lack depth and meaning. We may have many people to talk to, but no one in which to confide. Our interpersonal connections are less face-to-face and more digital. Our thumbs fly over the little screen to maintain superficial connections. We follow our kids through Facebook and not conversations over dinner. As we race through life, we no longer pause to give meaningful relationships a priority.

Our need for connection drives us to bury our authentic self and madly work on a more presentable self, a person who will be more connected. In the process, we push away any chance for real connection - connection with the true authentic self. We become nothing more than digital avatars. The social media image becomes more important than the actual but terrified authentic self. If the isolation becomes too painful to consider, at least, we live in a time of limitless distractions. If we would like to avoid the pain of loneliness, we can always buy a new computer game, join a club, or drown our pain in drugs or alcohol. This life is a life of quiet desperation. So, if we want to have more meaningful connections and revive the authentic self – how do we do that? We should not be afraid of isolation. To awaken the authentic self, we need a time of silence and solitude. We develop and mature in isolation; we uncover genius in solitude. If we feel we are continually observed, amid the noise and daily demands of life, there is no room to create brilliance. We have become so used to the sound of our busy world it causes anxiety to be without it – try turning off all electronic devices and sitting in a quiet room in complete silence for ten minutes. The silence is very uncomfortable because it is foreign. We have become comfortable with superficial, meaningless connections. For a moment, pause.

Pause and consider the following: Do you feel alone and isolated? Do you have others with whom you can confide? Are you working hard to create an image of yourself to be more acceptable to others? Are you authentic? What do you use as distractions from the pain of disconnection?

We live in an age of growing isolation amid limitless distractions and superficial connections.

We end up wasting a lot of our life trying to fight or change what we cannot change. You feel isolated and alone because you are isolated and alone. In other words, nobody knows you well, and you do not know anyone else very well. We do have connections, but the relationships are never good enough to eliminate the pain of isolation. You may be more distracted in a group, but you feel just as isolated in a group as you do on a desert island, at times even more isolated. You are not going to change this reality of life. Yes, there are things you can do to feel and be more connected, but in the end, you will still feel isolated.

Accept this reality for what it is: you may be the star quarterback in a stadium of 80,000 cheering fans, but who can you confide in - they care about how you perform, or what you can do for them, but do not care about you.

There will always be a distance in all relationships that will emphasize our awareness of felt isolation and aloneness. Remember, this is a universal experience, so be aware those you are closest too also feel isolated. Take time to consider their pain.

When considering this burden of isolation, you have several choices. You can fight the sense of isolation and pour all your energies into seeking connection - chances are all this will do is push away those from whom you are demanding relationship. This pursuit of relationship will require that you compromise your authentic self to be more acceptable. The process of compromising your authentic self through pretense will only leave you more aware of your isolation and aloneness.

You could deny the reality and just live with a sense something is not right. You can then feverishly seek out more ways to distract yourself - buy a new car, try a new sport, join a new club - the choices are endless and will allow you to remain busy, distracted, and empty for several lifetimes. This path of distraction is the path chosen by most people.

On the other hand, you could accept reality as the reality it is and let go of the burden. Letting go will take some work, but the work will lead to increased resilience and creativity. You may even get to the point where you can appreciate the reality for what it is.

If we want to get control of the burden of isolation and the fear of being alone, we will have to learn to appreciate this burden. In acknowledging it we are allowing ourselves to no longer be controlled by it, we can lessen its hold on us. Denying this burden through distractions or drowning in drugs and alcohol will not help. Avoiding this reality or running from it in fear will not help. We must learn to appreciate it to let it go. So, how do we do this? How can the existential burden of isolation become a blessing and not a curse?

First, we must pause to consider how it has been a burden in our lives and how that burden has impacted us and affected the crucial decisions we have made in the past. What did you do to lessen the pain of the load? What were the consequences of those decisions and the path they led you to follow? I can recall several abysmal life decisions I have made in the past as I was attempting to lessen the burden of felt isolation.

Felt isolation is painful. Solitary confinement is still a form of severe punishment. Prison is separation from those you care about - from those who care about you. Isolation can hurt deeply! Subjectively felt pain is selfish. It demands comfort. Drop a brick on your toe, and all you will be thinking about is your sore toe. Felt pain is a loud voice demanding all our focus and attention. The pain caused by felt isolation forces you to think about the isolation and the unfortunate state you are in - it makes you more self-centered and self-focused. The pain caused by perceived isolation, by making you more self-centered, increases the felt isolation. If, on the other hand, you accept the fact that all other humans share this burden, then it can be a point of connection and not a cause for separation. Shared pain is uniting; individual pain is isolating.

You can grow to realize this burden does not have to be feared, and you can appreciate it as something shared by all humans. This appreciation will allow you to experience a lessening of the weight, resilience will increase, and there will be a growing sense of freedom.

Now it is time to put this burden to work for our benefit.

The acceptance and appreciation of what this burden of isolation is can free you to grow in two significant ways. It can improve meaningful connections with others by recognizing we all share this burden, and it can strengthen authenticity by freeing you to embrace productive silence and solitude.

What you share with other humans can draw you together and not separate you. If you approach others looking for or demanding a connection from them, you will only increase your sense of isolation. If, on the other hand, you approach others, realizing they feel the pain of loneliness as much as you, and you are present to offer connection, then you are more likely to find a more meaningful relationship. Do not work to find others to connect to as a way of dismissing your felt isolation.

Look at how you can offer a meaningful connection. Focus on being more trustworthy, hold confidences, be kind, be honest, be humble, and remain thankful. You are more likely to get what you offer than to get what you demand. If you see the pain in others, it will lessen the impact of the pain and isolation you feel.

Put aside pretense. A manufactured, false image will only foster incorrect, meaningless, pressure-filled connections with others. If you want meaningful, genuine relationships, you need to be authentic. So, what does the path to authenticity look like in this crazy, fast-paced, noisy world? Only in silence and solitude will you find authenticity. In solitude is where isolation will make you stronger. Without silence and solitude, you will be a faint reflection of those around you, not thinking or believing for yourself, a finger puppet of the masses. I mean an isolated, lonely, finger puppet of the masses.

We are superficially connected in so many ways these days it is hard to picture solitude with silence. Why do we never leave our houses without our cell phones, or when we do, we feel something vital is missing - our constant conduit to the world, a short leash tied tightly around our neck. We need silence and solitude more now than ever before.

Solitude is taking time in a specific place with a deliberate purpose and plan. It is time to ponder and ask questions, it is a place we set aside, with a purpose of finding what you believe and stand for, and a life path that is not forced or pressured.

For solitude to be productive, you need time free from observation and distraction. You will need to unplug your electronic connection with the world.

There are several different forms of solitude with different purposes and focus.

There is a mind-numbing solitude, which is often more destructive than beneficial. We can find mind-numbing activities like drugs, alcohol, gambling, computer games, and excessive observation of sporting events or television. Mind-numbing solitude is a break from the everyday world, but the result is less resilience. Mind-numbing isolation is attractive because it provides a readily available separation from the pressures of the world with little personal investment. Over time this type of solitude loses its effectiveness and can cost you everything.

There is recreational solitude found in going for a walk or run, playing a sport, hiking in the woods, or sitting in a tree stand. If approached with a positive attitude, routine apparent mundane tasks like lawn mowing, floor cleaning, washing dishes, or car washing could be considered this type of recreational solitude. This type of solitude can be a real break from daily stresses as you have an opportunity to think through life issues without distractions from others. Recreational isolation can help improve your physical fitness and restore or maintain your resilience to a certain degree.

There is creative solitude found in activities like painting, photography, quilting, playing a musical instrument, or other creative activity. This type of solitude is another definite break from daily stressors and can also help restore your resilience.

The most valuable form of solitude is restorative solitude, where you sit in silence with pen and paper with a purpose and focus.

You will need a place where you can separate yourself from others and the world. This place needs to be easy to get to and free from interruption. If you find it very difficult to focus your thoughts because of distractions from your past, you may have to start with some therapeutic writing. Therapeutic writing is a way of setting aside past issues that weigh you down today. These could be past hurts, abuses, or injustices. To set aside these issues, take 30 minutes a day for four to five days, and write about the individual issue. This exercise will not eliminate the impact of past injustice, but, hopefully, it will help you to live more deliberately and not continue to live as a victim. If you live as a victim, you will live a powerless and ultimately meaningless and very isolated life. You do not want to live as a victim.

The goal of this time of solitude is to become more authentic. God only made one you and you are unique. No one else has your qualities or purpose. It would be a shame to neglect that uniqueness as you are working to gather appreciation from others, others who do not care.

Now that you have freed yourself from the burdens of past injustice, you can now focus on the present.

It is a time of separation from the thoughts, actions, words, and opinions of others. It is time to honestly and humbly evaluate and reevaluate. What are your core beliefs? What do you stand for? Who are you?

For restorative solitude to be productive, it needs to not turn into a time of fanciful daydreaming. It can be helpful to write your thoughts as a way of keeping your wandering mind in check. You will see in an upcoming chapter that there is a time for daydreaming, but this is not the time. The other sections in this book will give lots of areas of review to consider in this time of solitude. This is a time to find your purpose and meaning. A time to evaluate your choices and the consequences of those choices. A time to reflect on your mortality and the mortality of others. A time to ponder spiritual matters. A time to ask God to search your heart. What do you believe, and how is that evident in the way you live your life? I use this time to prayerfully consider passages in the Bible and how they apply to daily life.

Solitude time should be a time for reflection and contemplation and not a time for rumination over previous hurts and injustices. If you find these intrusive thoughts distracting you, then it may be time for more therapeutic writing.

It is not a race, take your time, remain focused but unpressured, and you will find, with God's guidance, that slowly your resilience, creativity, and authenticity will grow.

The burden of isolation is present because a part of the image of God in man is the capacity for an intimate relationship with God and humanity. If you continue to live with a fractured God-image you will live with the weight of isolation. There is a better way.

CHAPTER 5 - THE IMAGE – RELATIONSHIP

I n this chapter, we will look at the burden of isolation through a different lens. God's completed creation was "very good." Isolation is a heavy weight, and God did not create humans with the intent of carrying that weight. The experience of separation from God and our fellow man was not part of God's creation plan for humans. As I will show in this chapter, the experience of the burden of isolation is the result of a fracture that occurred in man's God-image when man disobeyed God.

Genesis 1:26-27 (AMP) records the creation of the first man. *"Then God said, "Let Us (Father, Son, Holy Spirit) make man in Our image, according to Our likeness [not physical, but a spiritual personality and moral likeness]; and let them have complete authority over the fish of the sea, the birds of the air, the cattle, and over the entire earth, and over everything that creeps and crawls on the earth. So God created man in His own image, in the image and likeness of God*

He created him; male and female He created them."

All of creation, light, darkness, earth, sky, waters, dry land, plants, trees, sun, moon, stars, seasons, days, years, fish, birds, and all living creatures came into being with God's Word. God spoke creation into existence, but not man. God created humanity differently than all the rest of creation. The physical substance of man came from the dust of the earth God had already spoken into existence. God's hands created and formed a man's body, and then man was given life and spirit by the breath of God. Humanity is unique among all creation, for no other part of creation was brought to life with the breath of God. Man is a body and a spirit, with an essence, both physical and spiritual.

God imprinted humanity with His image. This image of God is the essence of who we are as humans and is what makes us different than the rest of creation. The purpose of this image was to allow men to have an intimate relationship with God. When Adam turned his back on God in the garden, the image of God was not lost; it became fractured. What we now experience is a heavy burden. We know something is not right.

When I was in medical school, I managed to stay fit by running marathons and playing hockey. My marathon training gave me fitness and speed, that was an asset when it came to playing hockey. I was fit, and I was fast, but I was not skilled. I was a poor hockey player. One winter night in 1977, I had a great hockey-player night. I was faster than most nights, and I felt great. I was able to steal the puck from an opposing player and race down the ice with fantastic speed. I took my predictable, weak shot and hit the goalie in the chest, but unfortunately, I forgot to stop in time and hit the end boards with enough force to fracture my left lower leg. For the next several months, I painfully hobbled around with a cast and crutches. What was once my glory, my steadfast, fast legs, was now my weakness and a significant source of pain.

What happened to the image of God in us as people is very similar to my fractured leg experience. The pieces are all still present, but now they cause pain and anguish. The image is always the image, but the experience of the image has changed. What was to be our glory is still our glory, but now it is experienced as a burden. What was to be our strength is always our strength, but it now feels like a significant weakness.

If we live according to the God-given image, we are content, but if we live contrary to that image, the consequences are discontent, pain, turmoil, and a whole lot of wasted energy.

What does it mean to be made in the image of God? How are we to live according to that image?

There are several elements to the God-image. One of the components of the image of God is a capacity for relationship. We were made to have high-quality relationships with God and our fellow man.

We get so used to poor quality relationships; we don't even ask how to recognize a good quality relationship. The essential elements of a high-quality relationship are love, trust, and authenticity. If any of these elements is missing or weak, the relationship immediately begins to deteriorate. No relationship can stand for long on any one of these elements alone; they all need to be in place.

Love is considering others above yourself. It is not allowing yourself to be distracted by your struggles but choosing to be aware of the struggles and turmoil in someone else. Love is other-focused and not self-focused.

Trust is consistency in word and action; what you say is what you do.

Authenticity is consistency in word, action, and character; what you say and do is who you are with no pretense or deception.

God is a relational God. He is three in one; He is the father, Son, and Holy Spirit. God is three but relationally one. God is intimately connected to His creation and extends love and mercy towards humanity. As it says in Isaiah 54:10 (AMP), *"For the mountains may be removed and the hills may shake, But My lovingkindness will not be removed from you, nor will My covenant of peace be shaken, Says the Lord who has compassion on you."*

God's Word is His action, and His Word is His character. God is trustworthy and authentic. He is what He says He is.

As recorded in John 1:1 (AMP), *"In the beginning was the Word, and the Word was with God, and the Word was God Himself."*

He knows us better than we know ourselves and has not rejected us; Psalm 139:1-6 (AMP), *"O Lord, you have searched me [thoroughly] and have known me. You know when I sit down and when I rise up [my entire life, everything I do]; You understand my thought from afar. You scrutinize my path and my lying down, And You are intimately acquainted with all my ways. Even before there is a word on my tongue [still unspoken], Behold, O Lord, You know it all. You have enclosed me behind and before, and [You have] placed Your hand upon me. Such [infinite] knowledge is too wonderful for me; It is too high [above me], I cannot reach it."*

God demonstrates Himself by love, trust, and authenticity with the Godhead, towards humanity, and His creation. God is trustworthy; 2 Samuel 7:28 (NIV), *"Sovereign LORD, you are God! Your covenant is trustworthy, and you have promised these good things to your servant."*

God is authentic; He does not pretend to be something else or try to deceive. He is the "I AM." *"God said to Moses, "I Am Who I Am"; and He said, "You shall say this to the Israelites, 'I Am has sent me to you."* Exodus 3:14 (AMP)

Created humanity was to reflect God's quality of a relationship. Genesis 3:8 tells us that Adam and Eve recognized the sound of God walking in the garden. Humanity was to walk in harmony with God, to have a quality relationship with God and his fellow man.

Adam worked with God; he talked to God. God instructed him. Adam trusted God.

For some time, Adam did not hide from God; he remained authentic before God. We were created to be in harmony with one another to complement one another. *"Now the Lord God said, "It is not good (beneficial) for the man to be alone; I will make him a helper [one who balances him—a counterpart who is] suitable and complementary for him."* Genesis 2:18 (AMP) We were formed to complement each other and not to strive against one another. We were designed to enhance or emphasize the qualities of each other.

We were designed to love one another.
We were designed to trust and be trustworthy.
We were designed to be authentic and sincere.
We still bear God's image; we are to have high-quality relationships with God and our fellow man. God intends that we share these high-quality relationships with other image-bearers who are expressing the image of God they bear through love, trust-

worthiness, and authenticity. Without these relationships, we will experience discontentment.

God did not form the man out of the dust of the ground to create a zombie-like, perpetually contented creature who would worship and serve Him as a human puppet. Part of being made in God's image meant humanity had the ability and power for self-determination. God created us with a free-will. Adam used his free-will to set his course and turned his back on God. At the end of the sixth day, God looked at His creation and declared that it was "very good." Creation was free from sin, self-centeredness, rebellion, discontent, and death. Adam and Eve looked at God's creation and, like all men and women, since and they wanted more. Adam and Eve's act was a willful act of disobedience towards God, and the consequences were severe. Into God's "very good" creation entered, death, shame, blame, and the fear of God's presence. Humanity was left to solve their own problems. Humanity lost their intimate fellowship with God. They were removed from the garden but retained the memory of what they had lost. We still hold in our DNA the memory of that time in the garden; we know God created us for life in a "very good" creation. We know God made us for more, but because of sin and disobedience, we experience a life of pain, turmoil, and death.

The image of God in man was not lost, but the consequences

were devastating. God made us for high-quality, image-bearing relationships that we now experience as the burden of isolation. We feel very much alone; that no one understands us, and our problems are somehow unique, so it is up to us to solve them. We think our painful life experiences are more painful than anyone else's. We know God made us for a level and quality of relationship we are not experiencing. We are living with a fractured, unfulfilled image, and we feel very much alone.

Like Adam and Eve, we are aware of our inadequacies and spend our lives hiding from God and our fellow man. We are now afraid of God's presence as we desperately try to solve our unbearable situation.

We know we will face rejection if we are known for who we are, so we hide behind a projected image of who we think would be more acceptable. We live an exhausting life of pretense and deception. We give away our authenticity, we give away our image, and pick up an image we think would be more accepted. We live a lie hoping we will be less isolated and, in the process, increase our awareness of our isolation.

As we live our life of pretentious lies amongst others who are living pretentious lies, we learn that it is dangerous to trust. We read in Jeremiah 17:5 (AMP) that in this state, *"Cursed is the man who trusts in and relies on mankind, making [weak, faulty human] flesh his strength, and whose mind and heart turn away from the*

Lord." We now experience what should be high-quality relationships with distrust and disappointment.

The felt pain of isolation and poor-quality relationships leads to a life of self-protection and self-service. This life might look good from the outside, but deep down, it is self-serving. As we lose awareness of the pain and struggles of others, our love begins to grow cold, and our sense of isolation grows even more significant. The relational component of the image of God in our lives is fractured, and no matter how hard we try, or how loving we try to be, we cannot fix it.

We cannot fix this terminal problem on our own, but we have a loving God who has provided a path to restoration.

God's plan, through the sacrificial death and resurrection of His Son, is to provide a way back to Him and an opportunity for the healing of our fractured image.

Our rebellion against God came with a consequence; the consequence was death. God's provision for restoration required the death of His Son. His death was an unjust sacrifice; He did not deserve to die, we all deserved to die, but because of God's love, grace, and mercy, He died so we can now live and experience a restored relationship with God. Christ knew what it was to be human and what it was like to live in an evil world. He was tempted to turn from God in the same ways we have, yet He did not turn away from God. In Hebrews 4:15 (AMP), we read: *"For we do not have a High Priest who is unable to sympathize and understand our weaknesses and temptations, but One who has been tempted [knowing exactly how it feels to be human] in every respect as we are, yet without [committing any] sin."*

Christ's death was much more than execution by crucifixion. He experienced the pain and anguish of all our rebellion – He experienced all our physical and emotional distress, and yet He did not rebel or turn against God. He suffered a degree of pain no human has ever experienced.

Jesus experienced the full meaning of the burden of isolation. Someone who He trusted betrayed Him, betrayed with a kiss. His friends abandoned Him during His hour of greatest need; He was in anguish, and they were asleep. One of His closest friends denied that he knew Him, not once but three times. His disciples deserted Him and fled at the time of His arrest. He was falsely accused and mocked, and no one came to His defense. He experienced the physical pain of being forced to wear a crown of thorns, of being struck repeatedly, the weight of carrying the cross, and into His hands, and feet were driven the nails. He hung on the cross, alone, abandoned by His trusted friends, and yet He did not cry out. He only cried out when He experienced the most significant isolation possible, an experience no other man has ever experienced. He cried out in a loud voice, *"My God, My God, why have You forsaken Me?"* He was abandoned and forsaken by His Father, God, and yet He remained obedient. He suffered this for you and me so we can have a restored relationship with God.

In Colossians 1:21-22 (TPT), we read: *"Even though you were once distant from him, living in the shadows of your evil thoughts and actions, he reconnected you back to himself. He released his supernatural peace to you through the sacrifice of His own body as the sin-payment on your behalf so that you would dwell in His presence. And now there is nothing between you and Father God, for he sees you as holy, flawless, and restored,"*

We can now live, through faith, with a restored God-image.

Are you experiencing the impact of living with a relational fracture in your image? Do you feel like you are isolated and alone? Are you tired of living in a world of lies, where you feel like you cannot trust anyone? Are you exhausted from trying to live up to other's expectations that have caused you to abandon your authenticity? Are you tired of relating to people who are not authentic? Has self-centeredness got you discouraged and discontented? Are you filled with bitterness and greed? Are you longing for healthy relationships?

This cry is from the heart of your fractured image. We cannot deny that God made us for so much more. We are to live with a restored image, and we can live that way because of the work

Christ accomplished on the cross. Our part is to accept His gift of a restored life and then to begin to live. Live with a restored image. We can live with trust in God's promise in Jeremiah 29:11 (NKJV) *"For I know the thoughts that I think toward you, saith the LORD, thoughts of peace, and not of evil, to give you an expected end."* Unfortunately, the door to Eden is still locked. This side of heaven, we are left dealing with a fallen, rebellious world and the pain involved in living as a part of that world. This reality, however, is not an excuse for self-protective, self-centered living. With a restored, intimate relationship with God, we can show the world the experience of God's kind of relationship. If we do our part and live the God-image, God will provide all the comfort and direction we need while living in this crazy, upside-down world. We are free to be loving because He first loved us as in 1 Peter 4:8 (AMP), *"Above all, have fervent and unfailing love for one another, because love covers a multitude of sins [it overlooks unkindness and unselfishly seeks the best for others]."* And Ephesians 4:2-3 (AMP) *"with all humility [forsaking self-righteousness], and gentleness [maintaining self-control], with patience, bearing with one another in [unselfish] love. Make every effort to keep the oneness of the Spirit in the bond of peace [each individual working together to make the whole successful]."* God's kind of love is thinking of others more than thinking of ourselves; it is being more aware of the struggles of others than our felt pain. God-image relationship looks to give and not to get. In this relationship, there is contentment because we are living the way we are designed to live. 1 Corinthians 13:4-7 (AMP) describes this kind of love, *"Love endures with patience and serenity, love is kind and thoughtful, and is not jealous or envious; love does not brag and is not proud or arrogant. It is not rude; it is not self-seeking, it is not provoked [nor overly sensitive and easily angered]; it does not take into account a wrong endured. It does not rejoice at injustice, but rejoices with the truth [when right and truth prevail]. Love bears all things [regardless of what comes], believes all things [looking for the best in each one], hopes all things [remaining steadfast during difficult times], endures all things [without weakening]."*

We can now live freely with properly placed trust as described in Proverbs 3:5-6 (TPT), *"Trust in the Lord completely, and do not rely on your own opinions. With all your heart rely on him to guide you, and he will lead you in every decision you make. Become intimate with him in whatever you do, and he will lead you wherever you go."* Our issue is not so much with trustworthiness as it is in the faith we have in what, or whom we place our trust. The Bible makes it very clear to trust God and do not trust our fellow men. We need to trust only in Him who is faithful.

We do not need to fear authenticity or waste our life with exhausting pretense; God knows us thoroughly and still loves us. As stated in Psalm 139 (TPT), *"Lord, you know everything there is to know about me. You perceive every movement of my heart and soul, and you understand my every thought before it even enters my mind.*

You are so intimately aware of me, Lord. You read my heart like an open book and you know all the words I'm about to speak before I even start a sentence! You know every step I will take before my journey even begins." If we are free to be authentic with God, the most significant relationship in our lives, then we should be free to be more authentic in the rest of our life. We should not be afraid of solitude as it is a time we can ask God to search our hearts and reveal to us the areas where we need to repent and change. He will point out the areas that require cleaning; we need to get the broom and dustpan and begin sweeping.

As we walk with Him, we should be changing. Changing in a way that frees us to provide to others the kind of relationship God would desire. Our faith is communicated by how we relate. It is not our bumper stickers or tattoos; it is how we love others that they will recognize if we are indeed the children of God. Galatians 5:22 (TPT) lists the fruit of the Spirit, *"But the fruit produced by the Holy Spirit within you is divine love in all its varied expressions: joy that overflows, peace that subdues, patience that endures, kindness in action, a life full of virtue, faith that prevails, gentleness of heart, and strength of spirit."* We are not to consume this fruit in quiet solitude for our personal pleasure; they are to be nourishment for others and evidence of God's love towards us.

As we learn to trust God and walk as He would have us walk, in faith, we will see healing in our sense of isolation and loneliness. In Him, there is a resolution to the burden of isolation. In Him, there is contentment and God's kind of connectedness.

CHAPTER 6 - BURDEN OF MEANINGLESSNESS

I n Ecclesiastes 6:7 (MSG), we read, "We work to feed our appetites: meanwhile our souls go hungry." Hour after hour, day after day, we work our fingers to the bone to feed our hunger. A hunger that never seems to be satisfied. We end up exhausted and unfulfilled. We struggle to find meaning in who we are and what we do. We strive to find meaning, and in the process, lose contact with our value.

What is wrong? Why is there a disconnect between purposeful action and an expected result? The existential burden of meaninglessness often causes the disconnect.

Searching for meaning is a reality of human life. What it boils down to is the question - Why are we here, or why do we exist? What will make me worthwhile?

We look for meaning in labels, badges, legends, fantasies, legacy, and heritage.

We strive for labels hoping they will give us increased meaning and value. Tags like; officer, president, doctor, teacher, pastor, or your highness bring with them an increased degree of worth-whileness. Unfortunately, a name does not give you more value; a name carries with it a specific responsibility and expectation. If you are on the path to get a name to increase your sense of meaning, then you will find when you do get that label, it will be a disappointment.

Along with the label, you will also find all tags have qualifiers, and the qualifiers are much more important than the name. So, you may have gained the label of "the president," and the associated responsibilities, now you must focus on the qualifier because worse than not getting the name would be to get the name and the qualifier of being a "Bad" President. You will have to work harder to be a good president than you did to get the name of "the president." Labels may define specific roles in society and assigned responsibilities, and those responsibilities have degrees of meaning, but they do not provide any increased worth or value.

Badges are those external announcements to society that we have arrived. Badges are symbols not necessarily backed by any reality. If you drive a certain car, you are wealthy, even though it is an old car and it cost you everything you own. Badges are all around, from the clothes we wear to the car we drive to the way we comb our hair. Symbols make a statement of meaning but do not provide any meaningful increase in worth or value.

We look at legends to increase our worth. Legends are associations with others who we see as having more significant value. These associations may be with sports figures, celebrities, politicians, famous musicians, or people of power or wealth we see as being able to increase our sense of worth and value. Even just knowing a little secret about these individuals can increase my perceived sense of worth. Unfortunately, our legions have significant issues with value and worth themselves, and they are not the people we thought they were - in the long run, association with an esteemed someone else will not bring you an increased sense of value.

A trendy place to turn for an increased sense of meaning and value is fantasies. The world of imagination is the field mastered by media and the advertising industry. If I can make you believe a fantasy, I can sell you anything. We cling to the "if only" statements as we struggle with a sense of meaninglessness. "If only" I had – well you name it - a different house, a different job, a more significant bank account, a vacation home on the beach, a new motor home – and because it is out of reach you believe it would bring you the sense of value you desire. If you do end up acquiring the fantasy, you will end up disappointed - the new car now has its first scratch, the new job has increased demands and expectations, the increased wealth does not bring the sense of security you had hoped. Fantasies are valuable for the economy and the sale of lottery tickets, they keep people buying, but they only bring disappointment.

Another area where we attempt to cling to meaning and value is in the field of legacy. We try to hang on to past images of glory and success with the hope the momentarily increased sense will somehow last, but unfortunately, it does not last. Our trophies gather dust, and our medals and plaques get stored in a box we will never open. They are meaningless relics of a distant past.

Another area where we search for meaning is heritage. If I can find some ancestral hero, I will feel that I have greater worth. We search our family tree; we test our DNA; we cling to old family trinkets with the hope it will bring a greater sense of value. We search and search and find in every family tree there is good fruit and there is rotten fruit, our precious trinkets become clutter no one else wants, but we continue to reach to the past for a greater sense of worth in the present. Whether you are a descendant of Joan of Arc or Attila the Hun - it does not matter - your past heritage does not bring you higher or lesser worth today.

We are weighed down by the sense we have no value because who we are or what we do lacks the kind of meaning that makes us feel worthwhile. Feeling meaningless is a heavy burden to bear. We either carry it or learn how to deal with it. The first step in learning how to deal with this existential burden of meaninglessness is to acknowledge it exists and that it is a problem.

It is a part of our daily lives to ascribe meaning. Determination of meaning is subjective; what I determine to have meaning may have no meaning to anyone else. Determination of meaning is also relative; what has meaning to me today may have no meaning tomorrow; it all depends on the circumstances. If I am dying of thirst, a cup of water has more value than a bar of gold. Value and meaning are determined by what something represents. If you have two copper coins that each weigh the same, their value may be different because the image stamped on them is different. The value of each currency is the result of when and who minted the coins. We struggle to determine our meaning and how that meaning relates to our sense of value.

Our desires run deep and are a driving force in our lives. We desire for what we sense is lacking; some affirmation that our lives are achieving something of lasting value, yet our honest evaluation tells us all we do is meaningless and will have no lasting value. We keep chasing shadows. We reach for a future hope and, in the process, miss God's gifts that are available today.

The struggle with meaning is ultimately a struggle for comfort and contentment with the belief that if I have a purpose, then I will feel less discomfort and more peace. We incorrectly assume what we determine to be meaningful will give us an increased sense of value.

There are three general categories of meaning we can pursue.

We can pursue false meaning, transitory meaning, or ultimate meaning.

False meaning is the pursuit of immediate self-comfort and contentment. It is a type of endeavor that is often just a pleasant diversion and not helpful for long – often, it is the pursuit of activities for immediate pleasure that are harmful. In the long run, the pursuit of food, drink, drugs, money, power, or any other action considered immediately pleasurable is not connected to any form of lasting meaning. This type of meaning is very superficial; it is a distraction from the turmoil and troubles of life. It is a desperate attempt to cover the sensation and discomfort of feeling meaninglessness and worthless, or to soothe the pain of an existential crisis.

Transitory meaning is the pursuit of long-term self-comfort and contentment. It is where the quest is not destructive, but neither does it give any lasting meaning or purpose. Developing skills, achieving success, receiving an education, pursuing health interests, may not cause harm: they do keep us busy and distracted but do not provide any ultimate or lasting meaning. We falsely interpret the accolades received for accomplishment as attributing meaning and value. This positive sensation is fleeting. We devote all our time, energy, and emotion into achieving the most difficult of goals, with the belief the more out of reach an accomplishment is, the more it will give us a sense of value. Many people will spend their life trying to achieve the impossible, and if they realize their goal, they find they are disappointed because the achievement did not bring the desired result of a sense of lasting worth. In the end, this results in exhaustion and disappointment.

Ultimate meaning is where the pursuit of comfort and contentment is on behalf of others. You find ultimate meaning in a relationship with something or someone greater than us. This ultimate meaning transcends the other issues of relationship, mortality, and free choice and can put those other areas into a more realistic perspective. This ultimate type of meaning is rare because it requires faith.

We end up wasting a lot of our life trying to fight or change what we cannot change. We struggle with the burden of meaninglessness because it is part of us. We all want to know we have value and who we are and what we do is not meaningless. We always compare and attribute different values and meanings throughout the day. We use this ability to evaluate and contrast when it comes to ourselves, what we possess, and the tasks we perform. It is excruciating when we realize our actions and accomplishments are meaningless, with no value or purpose because that is most often the reality. This existential burden of meaninglessness drives us to deny the facts and distract us through meaningless, distracting activities. We are now back to that life of quiet desperation.

Our search for meaning and value is a search for some action, attribute, or quality within our control that could somehow lessen the pain and discomfort of isolation, minimize the terror of our mortality, alleviate the angst of free choice and spiritual emptiness.

We live with the belief there is something we can do or say that will give our felt meaningless lives some sense of value. So, we work hard to pursue positions, accomplishments, physical attributes, memberships in the best clubs, entertainment, or even personal sacrifice, to give ourselves a value boost. All to no avail, we still end up feeling meaningless. Pursuing meaning and value seem to push it further and further away.

When we pour all our energies into achieving a self-defined meaningful result to feel worthwhile, we only make the problem of meaninglessness worse. Goals are essential in life, they give our lives direction and purpose, but we must be cautious when we overvalue results. Results are not always within our control. To focus on results leads to a life of disappointment because it becomes a life of constant comparison - there will always be others with better results. Even if you only compare yourself with yourself, your ability to achieve a specified result will eventually become more difficult, if not impossible, as you age. Focusing on results to give you a greater sense of worth is also discouraging because, even if you achieve the desired effect, you will find that it can never bring you the sensation of value you so wish. Another problem with pursuing results to give you a greater sense of importance is when you focus too intently on a result, you have sacrificed the benefit of today for an anticipated future occurrence. You lose track of the joys and creativity present today in the process – you achieve satisfaction based only on the next result, and then the pleasure only lasts for a short period. In other words, to give meaning to an expected result, to attain a sense of value or worth will only steal your joy and contentment, kill your creativity, and

65

destroy your awareness of your true worth. Your song remains unsung.

Do not forget, the people you see as having meaning and value look back at you with their feelings of meaninglessness, believing that through your meaningless activities, you have achieved worth. We all want to feel significant, that who we are and what we do has some value. The harder we try to attain comfort, the more discomfort we experience.

Once we have accepted this burden for what it is and that it is present in every human, we can get to the point where it can be appreciated. So, how do we do this? How do we learn to understand the burden of meaninglessness? How can meaninglessness become a blessing?

Firstly, we must realize there is a difference between meaning and value. What is the difference between meaning and value when it comes to how we see ourselves? Meaning is subjective, while value is objective. Meaning is a focus on what you do, and value is a focus on who you are. Meaning is direction focused; it focuses on where you are going, where value is determined by where you are in the present. Meaning is what you know and believe; value is who you are. Meaning looks back to the past and forward to the future; value looks to the present. Meaning is subjective, where value is objective. Meaning fosters pride, where value encourages humility. Meaning rests on what I create, but my value rests in the awareness that God created me. Meaning promotes status or social position where value fosters purpose. Meaning is data-based, where value is faith-based. Meaning focuses on the observable gain, where value focuses on enrichment and life direction more than specific achievements.

Once we realize we all carry this burden and no single individual act can bring us the meaning and value our soul longs for, then we can be free from the pressure to find meaning where meaning does not exist.

When we place the demand for meaning on any specific action or quality, we only increase our discomfort. This knowledge can free us from attempting to diminish the feeling of meaninglessness through accomplishments, status, physical attributes, acquaintances, memberships, knowledge, wisdom, sacrifice, spiritual endeavors, or notoriety. The increased sense of value from all these endeavors is weak and fleeting. You are now free to approach your life and activities in a way that can bring real peace and contentment.

The burden of meaninglessness does not have to weaken you; it can make you stronger. How can this be possible? How can the weight of meaninglessness strengthen you? No activity, accomplishment, or possession, no matter how meaningful you determine it to be, will give you the value or sense of worth you so desperately desire. So, what are we to do?

Ecclesiastes 5: 19-20 (NLT) has some good advice regarding meaning and significance. It states: *"To enjoy your work and accept your lot in life – this is indeed a gift from God. God keeps such people so busy enjoying life that they take no time to brood over the past."*

What this verse is saying is that there is joy in today's work if we are willing to accept our lot - or current results.

Think back to the example of the coins of various value because of the image on the coin. Like the coin, our worth is not our substance; it is not our flesh and blood or what we can do with our flesh and blood; it is what God has stamped on our soul; the image of the creator. The value comes from His image. We have an inherent value not based on who we are or what we do but, on whose image we bear. An essential element of the image of our creator is creativity. The existential burden of meaninglessness will steal, destroy, and kill our God-given creativity. Our creative God-image is the part of us that is valuable and meaningful and a gift of God to all humanity. You are worthwhile; you have a song to be sung. You and your song are a gift to all of humanity. Do not throw this gift away, trying to achieve some warped sense of meaning. Take time to evaluate where you determine your real sense of worth. If we focus our creative energies on the task before us today and not the results of completing that task, we will free ourselves to experience joy and contentment without having to place a value judgment on an accomplished job. God's gift is the freedom and ability to enjoy your work and the fruits of your labor. The type of work you do is not as important as your freedom to apply your creative energies to enjoy that work.

My grandfather was a great example of living this kind of blessed life. He was not a wealthy or highly educated man. He grew up in a Russian speaking community in Canada that immigrated because of religious persecution. He only managed to get to third grade in school and had to teach himself to read English. I had the privilege of building two homes with him. I learned a lot from him by observing how he lived his life. He never saw a challenge as impossible, nor did he try to avoid a task. He did not rejoice over the finished product – he just applied his creative self to every daily problem. His joy-filled but straightforward life had a positive impact on many people. His legacy was how he lived his life.

We will experience value, meaning, and contentment if we: focus on the process and not the product, our attitude and not our achievement, our creativity and not our creation, our op-

RICHARD ARTHUR HINDMARSH MD

portunities, and not our trials.

Take some time, find that place of solitude and ask yourself the following questions - be sure to write your answers.

To what are you looking to feel worthwhile? Where do you find your value? What does it mean to be creative? Do you give too much meaning to results? Have you found joy in your work? How do you approach your day? Have you found your "song"? Are you singing your song? What does it mean that God made you in His image?

Once we are free from the belief that an accomplishment will give us meaning, we can focus on what can provide us with joy – the creative process and living the image of God. As a community, if you are free to sing your song, we will all be enriched. Our actual value is in the reality that we are valuable to God, so valuable that He gave His Son to die for us to restore our relationship with Him.

CHAPTER 7 - THE IMAGE – SUBSTANTIAL VALUE

W hat is the meaning of life? Why am I here? What is the purpose of my existence? We all struggle with the burden of meaninglessness. The struggle with meaning is a cry about our perceived value. The battle to find meaning is the battle to find worth.

In God's kingdom, God determined our value and worth. Our created purpose is to have a quality relationship with our creator and be co-creators. He has placed His image within us, and He is a loving creator who has shown us mercy and grace. He sent His only Son to die for us to allow for a restoration in our relationship to Him. He sent us His Holy Spirit to guide and comfort us, so we could tolerate living in a fallen, rebellious world.

In Psalm 144:3 (NIV), we read, *"Lord, what is man that You take notice of him? Or the son of man that You think of him?"* How would your life change today if you lived as an expression of this awareness? God loves you even more than you love yourself.

The God who created the universe and all it contains thinks of you.

In the summer of 1979, our extended family gathered for an exceptional event. My great-grandmother was celebrating her 100th birthday - the small Canadian town where she lived closed down for the day. The entire family and community came together at the local hockey rink that had been decorated and equipped with special sound equipment. We all gathered and eagerly awaited the telephone call from the Queen of England, wishing great grandma a happy 100th birthday. Now, we knew the Queen did not know any of us or, for that matter, even cared about any of us; she just followed the instructions provided by her advisers and made the call. The call came through as expected, we were all happy, and the memory lingers to this day. How much more should we be affected by the reality that the God of this universe thinks about each of us? He knows us and He cares about each of us. This truth is worth pausing to consider. Take time to meditate about this truth; it will change your life.

The breath of God gave a newly created man something special and separated him from the rest of creation. God gave us a spirit and His image. We are not the same as other animals; we have a different value, meaning, and purpose. Life is a gift from God, and human life is sacred. All human life is sacred. We need to see our experience and the lives of others from God's point of view and not from our own selfish perspective.

We possess God's image. We have a God-given spirit that is not present in the rest of creation. Humans are special. As recorded in Genesis 2:7 (AMP) *"Then the Lord God formed [that is, created the body of] man from the dust of the ground, and breathed into his nostrils the breath of life; and the man became a living being [an individual complete in body and spirit]."* We breathe today because of that first God-given breath.

We have a special place in creation. We are to rule, cultivate, and preserve. We are to be complementary to each other. In Genesis 1:26 (AMP) we read: *"Then God said, "Let Us (Father, Son, Holy Spirit) make man in Our image, according to Our likeness [not physical, but a spiritual personality and moral likeness]; and let them have complete authority over the fish of the sea, the birds of the air, the cattle, and over the entire earth, and over everything that creeps and crawls on the earth."* We have the authority and responsibility other elements of creation do not have. We have a position of honor as recorded in Psalm 8:5 (AMP) *"Yet You have made him a little lower than God, And You have crowned him with glory and honor."*

The relationship between God and man is a theme throughout the entire Bible. We are to walk with God, talk with God, and have intimacy with God. We have examples in the Old Testament with Adam, Abraham, Isaac, Jacob, Moses, David, and the many others who sought God. We also have multiple New Testament examples. Man is complete only when he is in right relationship to God. God desires to be in contact with humanity.

God knows all there is to know about us. He knows us better than we know ourselves. As written in Psalm 139:1 - 2 (TPT), *"Lord, you know everything there is to know about me. You perceive every movement of my heart and soul, and you understand my every thought before it even enters my mind."* God knows us thoroughly. He knows our strengths, and He knows our weaknesses. He knows when we are authentic, and He knows when we are deceptive. He knows when we are generous, and He knows when we are selfish. He knows when we are good, and He knows when we are evil. If we were to know anyone this well, we would have valid reason to reject them, but God, who knows us ultimately has not rejected us. We are the species who killed His Son, and He is the God who let His Son suffer and die so we could have a restored relationship with Him. This truth is just too much to comprehend fully.

He knows us, and yet He loves us. Even amid our open rebellion and rejection, He still loves us. After Adam and Eve rebelled against God in the garden, God continued to talk to them. God is the one who made them a covering more suitable than sowed fig leaves. There were severe consequences to the act of rejection of God in the garden of Eden, but the loss of God's love was not one of the results. This love of God is not dependent on race, skin color, gender, or social status. The love of God extends to all, regardless of how good or evil. Peter said in Acts 10:34 (TPT), *"Now I know for certain that God doesn't show favoritism with people but treats everyone on the same basis."* It does not matter how lovable or unlovely we are; God still loves us. It does not matter how much we feel loved by others; God still loves us. *"For this is how much God loved the world—he gave his one and only, unique Son as a gift. So now everyone who believes in him will never perish but experience everlasting life."* John 3:16 (TPT) Human love is most often based on merit; God's kind of love is present just because you exist. It is impossible as mere humans to comprehend this type of love. This type of love should motivate us to serve Him and then be free to show that love to others.

"Lord, what is man that You take notice of him? Or the son of man that You think of him?" Psalm 144:3 (AMP), The God of this universe, thinks of us. God did not create the universe and humanity and then leave for a prolonged vacation. The God who created and sustains everything is concerned enough about you to be thinking about you right now. We are dull, weak, self-

centered, humans, and yet we are valued by Him, and we should be living aware of this value.

God created a perfect world for Adam and Eve. They had an intimate relationship with God and could work as co-creators in God's perfectly designed world. They had a relationship with God with meaning and purpose. Yet, what they experienced was not enough. Adam and Eve, like the rest of us, wanted more, they chose to disobey God to gain exclusive insight and awareness. In this action, man turned his back on God and chose his own way. *"And when the woman saw that the tree was good for food, and that it was delightful to look at, and a tree to be desired in order to make one wise and insightful, she took some of its fruit and ate it; and she also gave some to her husband with her, and he ate. Then the eyes of the two of them were opened [that is, their awareness increased], and they knew that they were naked, and they fastened fig leaves together and made themselves coverings."* Genesis 3:6-7 (AMP) This act of rebellion awakened man's self-condemning consciousness. Shame, guilt, blame and fear now entered man's experience of life. One act gave our conscious a loud voice, and since that time, we have tried to eat, drink, smoke, or inject something else to silence that voice. We are not the victims of the choices Adam and Eve made; we all would have made the same choice.

We are now living with a fractured value-image. We gave away the awareness of our unique value. We still sense that we have significant value but have lost the appropriate context for that awareness. We now hide from God and search for a sense of value anywhere else.

Our fractured value-image is now self-centered and focused on self-protection. We now hide from God as did Adam and Eve in Genesis 3:8-12 (AMP) *"And they heard the sound of the Lord God walking in the garden in the cool [afternoon breeze] of the day, so the man and his wife hid and kept themselves hidden from the presence of the Lord God among the trees of the garden. But the Lord God called to Adam, and said to him, "Where are you?" He said, "I heard the sound of You [walking] in the garden, and I was afraid because I was naked; so, I hid myself." God said, "Who told you that you were naked? Have you eaten [fruit] from the tree of which I commanded you not to eat?" And the man said, "The woman whom You gave to be with me—she gave me [fruit] from the tree, and I ate it."* We did not lose the value-image, but the wonder and positive experience of the image were lost. The experience of our value as God-created and God-loved morphed into guilt, shame, blame, and self-protection. Awareness of personal value and significant worth was lost, so we now believe we must do something to regain a sense of worth.

With humanity's rebellion, our role in creation also shifted dramatically. Mankind was moved out of God's garden and into a world of chaos and disorder as recorded in Genesis 3:13-19 (AMP) *"Then the Lord God said to the woman, "What is this that you have done?" And the woman said, "The serpent beguiled and deceived me, and I ate [from the forbidden tree]." The Lord God said to the serpent, "Because you have done this, you are cursed more than all the cattle, and more than any animal of the field; On your belly you shall go, and dust you shall eat All the days of your life. "And I will put enmity (open hostility) Between you and the woman, and between your seed (offspring) and her Seed; He shall [fatally] bruise your head, and you shall [only] bruise His heel." To the woman He said, "I will greatly multiply Your pain in childbirth; In pain you will give birth to children; Yet your desire and longing will be for your husband, and he will rule [with authority] over you and be responsible for you." Then to Adam the Lord God said, "Because you have listened [attentively] to the voice of your wife, and have eaten [fruit] from the tree about which I commanded you, saying, 'You shall not eat of it'; The ground is [now] under a curse because of you; In sorrow and toil you shall eat [the fruit] of it All the days of your life. "Both thorns and thistles it shall grow for you, and you shall eat the plants of the field. "By the sweat of your face You will eat bread Until you return to the ground, for from it you were taken; For you are dust, and to dust you shall return."*

Humanity now looks for a tangible sense of meaning and purpose apart from a relationship with God, but no matter how hard we try, we will not succeed. Our God-breathed image will only be content with a sense of value in a restored relationship with God.

Men live as if they can successfully hide from God or deny His existence. In the process of rejecting God, men turn to other idols to give them a sense of meaning. What we worship is what defines our sense of worth. As recorded in Romans 1:19-23 (TPT), humanity is still aware, through all their layers of denial, that a loving God exists; *"In reality, the truth of God is known instinctively, for God has embedded this knowledge inside every human heart. Opposition to truth cannot be excused based on ignorance, because from the creation of the world, the invisible qualities of God's nature have been made visible, such as his eternal power and transcendence. He has made his wonderful attributes easily perceived, for seeing the visible makes us understand the invisible. So then, this leaves everyone without excuse. Throughout human history, the fingerprints of God were upon them, yet they refused to honor him as God or even be thankful for his kindness. Instead, they entertained corrupt and foolish thoughts about what God was like. This left them with nothing but misguided hearts, steeped in moral darkness. Although claiming to be super-intelligent, they were in fact shallow fools. For only a fool would trade the unfading splendor of the immortal God to worship the fading image of other humans, idols made to look like people, animals, birds, and even creeping reptiles!"*

Now, in times of trouble and turmoil instead of turning to a loving God for support and direction, humanity looks for help from their possessions or their "emotional-support pet." What fools we are!

Even if your focus is on a new car, job, relationship, or pet as a means of gaining some meaning, God is still thinking about you. You may have turned away from Him, but He has not turned away from you.

God not only thinks of you and loves you; He has made way for you to return to a relationship with Him. He has provided the way, even though there is nothing in us that is deserving. *"Even though you were once distant from him, living in the shadows of your evil thoughts and actions, He reconnected you back to himself. He released his supernatural peace to you through the sacrifice of his own body as the sin-payment on your behalf so that you would dwell in his presence. And now there is nothing between you and Father God, for he sees you as holy, flawless, and restored,"* Colossians 1:21-22 (TPT)

God's restoration plan provides for the healing of our fractured value-image. A renewed relationship with God means I can now experience my substantial value in Him, and not in my selfish efforts. My worth does not come from who I am or what I do; my worth comes from God Himself.

I can now rest in this God-given value and no longer need to spend every moment of my life desperately searching for a sense of meaning. There is incredible freedom in realizing that my possessions, relationships, accomplishments, physical attributes, and affiliations may give me some warped knowledge of meaning but have no bearing on my true worth. If we live in the God-given value-image, there is no pressure to perform for the sake of acquiring value or purpose. We can rest in Him!

I am now free to work hard, be productive, and creative without being driven to find meaning or continually live with the burden of a lack of felt meaning. Living with my awareness of value secure in my relationship with God, means I am free to live in a way that can now have purpose and meaning. I can focus on a task without requiring a sense of meaning from the results. I am free from a life of self-service and can live the life God intended.

While He walked among men, men threatened Jesus' value-image. He experienced the same temptation to seek value, meaning, and purpose apart from His relationship to God.

He humbled Himself and became a man.

He lived among self-centered men and was judged by them. They should have valued Him, but instead, they judged Him unfairly.

He was mocked and ridiculed, and they attacked His God-given purpose.

He had a message of salvation for the world, but He was only listened to by a few. The miracles He performed were not to make a name for himself but to serve those who cried out in need. He came as a representation of God's love, and the world rejected Him.

"For we do not have a High Priest who is unable to sympathize and understand our weaknesses and temptations, but One who has been tempted [knowing exactly how it feels to be human] in every respect as we are, yet without [committing any] sin." Hebrews 4:15 (AMP) He knows our struggle with value, meaning, and purpose. He was tempted by Satan to act on His own behalf to acquire meaning; in Matthew 4:1-11 (TPT) we read about this temptation; *"Afterward, the Holy Spirit led Jesus into the lonely wilderness in order to reveal his strength against the accuser by going through the ordeal of testing. And after fasting for forty days, Jesus was extremely weak and famished. Then the tempter came to entice him to provide food by doing a miracle. So, he said to Jesus, "How can you possibly be the Son of God and go hungry? Just order these stones to be turned into loaves of bread." He answered, "The Scriptures say: Bread alone will not satisfy, but true life is found in every word, which constantly goes forth from God's mouth." Then the accuser transported Jesus to the holy city of Jerusalem and perched him at the*

highest point of the temple and said to him, "If you're really God's Son, jump, and the angels will catch you. For it is written in the Scriptures: He will command his angels to protect you and they will lift you up so that you won't even bruise your foot on a rock." Once again Jesus said to him, "The Scriptures say: You must never put the Lord your God to a test." And the third time the accuser lifted Jesus up into a very high mountain range and showed him all the kingdoms of the world and all the splendor that goes with it. "All of these kingdoms I will give to you," the accuser said, "if only you will kneel down before me and worship me." But Jesus said, "Go away, enemy! For the Scriptures say: Kneel before the Lord your God and worship only him." At once the accuser left him, and angels suddenly gathered around Jesus to minister to his needs." Jesus lived the God-image. His value was secure in His relationship with God and not in His accomplishments. He was free to love and serve.

His ultimate act of service was to carry all our sin, grief, guilt, shame, and pain on the cross.

How do you know you are living with a fractured value-image? What does it feel like to live with a broken value-image? Why carry a weight you do not need to carry? The following are a few clues to life's experience with a fractured value-image.

One way to determine if you have issues with your value is to pass your self-evaluation through the filter of pets, possessions, presidents, and peasants. If your pet dog is valued as a person or has greater importance than the people in your life, then you have significant issues with your sense of value. Yes, your pet cat and dog are unique, they are part of God's beautiful creation, but if you view them as your "fur-children" that makes you no more than their hairless parent. You are worth much more than that.

If you strive to gain and protect your possessions, and they have a value higher than the people in your life, you have issues with your significance. If you believe there are people of more excellent value in God's eyes (presidents or people of prominence) then you have problems with your sense of worth. We are all different with different strengths and roles, but we all carry the same value in God's eyes. If you believe you are more esteemed than others because of their lifestyle or choices (peasants), then, in the process, you are devaluing your worth. In God's kingdom, humanity is extraordinary, with much higher value and significance than animals, possessions, or people of high or low status or esteem.

A current struggle with meaning and purpose is a clue you are struggling with a fractured value-image. Each new phase in life can be a time where this struggle becomes most apparent. Are you asking yourself the questions: Why am I here? What is my purpose? What is life's meaning? Or are you struggling with how meaningless things seem to be: you have worked hard, you are exhausted, but for what purpose. As I write this chapter, I am in the pre-retirement phase of life. If my value were in being a physician, I would be facing a significant life crisis with the transition. If you want to avoid disaster, you will need to be secure in the source of your value. Our value is not what we do, what we look like, who we know, or what we think we own.

Another clue that your value-image may be fractured is deep dissatisfaction with yourself. Are you troubled that you are too young, too old, too short, too tall, too fat, too skinny, too ugly, too beautiful, too weak or too strong? The list of dissatisfaction categories is limitless. This dissatisfaction comes from living your life by comparison. Are you constantly comparing yourself to others? If you are in this pit of discontent, you are living with a fractured value-image. God loves you just as you are, and that should be good enough.

Are you living with constant pressure to do more? Are you focused more on doing than being? The value-image God gave us has nothing to do with all our doing. We need to learn to rest in God's criteria for value and worth.

Do you feel you will never have enough? Do you think you need to gain and own more to feel a greater sense of value? The source of this drive to own and possess comes from a fractured value-image. Our understanding of security and our awareness of importance are closely aligned. If you are secure in your sense of worth, you will be confident in the belief that God will provide all you need.

Are you spending a lot of energy attempting to climb up the corporate ladder? Do you spend your days preoccupied with self-promotion? There is nothing wrong with advancement, but endless self-promotion is evidence of a fractured value-image. If your purpose is to be noticed or gain affirmation, you will end up discouraged and depressed.

Have you lost your sense of inherent value? If you look back on your life at times where you felt you were more aware of your value-image than you do now, then it may be time for an honest inventory. We need to live honestly, daily asking God to exam our hearts and then have the humility and courage to change what needs changing.

Do you give more value to achievement than to service? An achievement-oriented life is a sign of a fractured value-image. We should focus our actions on service. When you are at a point in your life when you wonder what you should be doing, like looking for a job or choosing an educational path, don't ask what you should do, ask who you should serve. Contentment comes from a life of service.

How often do you refer to yourself in regular day-to-day conversations? Communication filled with "I" and "me" is evidence of a fractured value-image and a focus on self-service and self-promotion.

Human life is sacred. We are very different than the rest of creation. We were given, by God Himself, a form and a spirit. We carry His image, and that is sacred. All human life is holy, from the unborn to the debilitated elderly to your annoying neighbor. All life is holy, and all people are struggling. If you become so self-absorbed that you lose this awareness or are more concerned with the status of your pet cat than the soul of your enemy, then you are living with a fractured value-image. Lord, save us from ourselves and our preoccupation with ourselves!

The good news is that we do not have to continue this path of self-absorbed insecurity. God has provided a way to a restored value-image through the sacrifice of his Son.

With this restored image, your value is secure.

You can set aside all your wasted energy, trying to gain a sense of worth by your actions. Why live in a constant state of meaningless exhaustion?

You are now free to live as you were initially intended to live. You are free to serve and protect as God designed you. Live the image.

CHAPTER 8 - BURDEN OF FREE CHOICE AND RESPONSIBILITY

I n Deuteronomy 30:19 (NLT) God instructed the people that: "Today I have given you the choice between life and death, between blessings and curses. Now I call on heaven and earth to witness the choice you make. Oh, that you would choose life, so that you and your descendants might live!"

Our life is filled with daily choices – too numerous to count. We choose a path, and the path leads to a result. The result is the consequence of the decision we have made. It is our choice – select the road leading to life or the road leading to death. The decision is your responsibility.

In this chapter, I will be dealing with the existential burden of free choice and personal responsibility. We are in the privileged and yet, terrifying position of being able to create who we are through the choices we make. The frightening part is it is our personal and individual responsibility to make those choices.

If you abandon your responsibility by living as a victim, with bitterness, fear, or anger, you are giving up your power and the ability to create a new you. It is ultimately your choice, a choice that should be a freedom and not a hindrance.

This chapter is not a philosophical debate on free will. Whether you are a determinist, a compatibilist, or a libertarian, you will still have to choose many times today, and those choices will make a difference in your life; they will affect your present and future life experience. You will make choices today, and you will have to be responsible for the consequences and outcomes of those choices.

The first step in learning how to deal with this existential burden of free choice and personal responsibility is to acknowledge it exists and that it is a problem. Our life is the sum of the choices we make, and we make thousands of them every day. We face hundreds of immediate daily options, from what we will have for breakfast, to what clothes we will wear, to what we will do with our day. We make choices about our future, like what we will do for our education or work, to where we will go for vacation this year, that is, if we have chosen to set aside enough money throughout the year to be able to afford a vacation. We decide where we will live, what we will believe, who we will marry, and on and on. We even get to choose a lot of our emotional responses, whether we will be angry or bitter or decide just to let things go and be happy. Our life is a massive flow chart of decisions leading to where we are today. What it boils down to is this burden of free choice, and personal responsibility is a matter of what we choose to do with what we have. To get a better handle on this burden in a way that we can make it work for us, we need to be aware of what we have, and what options we have when it comes to choosing what to do with what we have.

So, what do we have? What we have can be broken down into the four categories of person, place, things, and time.

What do we have as a person? We have our personality, our core beliefs, and our physical body - this is our person. Within this category of "my person," there is room for limitless choice. What is your personality? How can you determine how your character will show itself? What components of your personality would you like to change? What are your core beliefs? You need to take time to consider what your core beliefs are as they are the main factor in determining your life's direction. You have many choices regarding your physical body. Unfortunately, we all have limitations to our potential when it comes to fitness, we cannot all be Olympic athletes or world-class swimmers, but as you sit here today, you are as fit and as fat as you have chosen to be. You are responsible for everything you put in your mouth and accountable for what you do for exercise. Sorry, but it is not your thyroid or the size of your bones, if you are fat, it is because you have overeaten many times and that was your choice. Another part of our personality that often gets neglected is our dreams. Our imagination and dreams bring about new directions and inventions, often making the world a better place. We should choose to allow ourselves time to dream.

The next category is the category of place. What is our place? Our place is the space we occupy and our defining titles, which is the space we employ in the lives of others. It is where we live, where we work, and how others define us. We live and work in an established community in a specific country at a time in history. We define ourselves by titles like a friend, neighbor, husband, wife, teacher, banker, sister, brother, son, or daughter. If you take the time to consider this list of titles, it will be extensive. What place do you want to occupy? What choices will you have to make to occupy that chosen space? What titles are used by others to define you? Options in this area will end up consuming most of your time, so be careful how and what you choose.

The category of things is also pervasive. It is the category of

RICHARD ARTHUR HINDMARSH MD

what we feel we own. It is our resources, our talents, our job, our family, and our immediate responsibilities. We face multiple daily choices as to what we are to do with what we own. This choice is the area where we are most aware of the importance and demand of daily choices and decisions. What resources do you have? How do you plan to use those resources? What do you plan to do with your talents?

The next category is the category of time. We all have an allotment of time, how we choose to spend it will be the most significant factor in the outcome of our life. We measure the quantity of our life by years when it would serve us better to measure the amount by days. We should approach each day as if it is a new year. What and how you choose today will have a more significant impact on your life than what you plan to do in the distant next year. If you choose wisely the path for your day, the year will take care of itself. Yes, long term plans are necessary, but it is what you decide to do with the day that will determine if you achieve those plans. Today is my 24,265th day. We should live counting our days and not counting our years. This day is a gift – spend it wisely. We make a lot of wrong assumptions regarding time and how to spend it wisely. There needs to be a balance with work time and rest time, active time, and meditative time. We need time to push ahead and time to step back. We are wrong to assume it takes massive amounts of consecutive time to accomplish something of value. The reality is we can achieve a lot with the regular, daily utilization of small allotments of time.

It is best to view all these components of person, place, things, and time as potential bearing seeds. For example, we all have a handful of time, where we choose to plant those "time seeds" will determine a lot of what happens in our life. It is a worthwhile exercise to spend some quiet time in solitude to consider and evaluate what you have, what seeds are in your pocket - it is a good idea to write them down and ponder the best way to plant and care for those precious seeds.

What can we do with these seeds? What are our options? As an example, let's say you have just received an unexpected thousand-dollar check from the IRS for an overpayment of your last year's taxes. What can you do with that check? Firstly, you may decide to do nothing, after all, it was utterly unexpected, maybe it's a fake. So, you determine the best thing is to do nothing, leave it in the envelope. You have another option; you may decide to throw it away. This option may not be the wisest choice, but it is still an option. Another option would be to acknowledge it as legitimate but to treat it carelessly and just put it in a drawer with the plan to take it to the bank sometime in the future. Another choice would be to take it to the bank and then treat it casually, forgetting it is in your account. You may also decide to cash the check and take the money home and just put it aside for some future need. You may choose to give it away to be used by others, or you may decide to invest it and patiently wait for it to grow. Whatever you end up deciding to do, it is your choice and your responsibility to make that choice. You have multiple options for what you choose to do with that IRS check, just like you have numerous options for all the other seeds you possess. What freedom and potential! I get to choose what to do, what direction my life will go. So, where is the problem?

The issue is these free choices don't feel very free much of the time, and we end up wasting a lot of our life trying to fight or change what we cannot change. The following are some of the factors that make a free choice fell like a burden.

Firstly, it puts you in the driver's seat; your choices are your responsibility. We may not have an issue with free choice, but we do have problems with being personally responsible, especially when things do not go as planned. Yes, you do get to choose what direction you go, but what you don't get to choose is the consequences of that choice. You must own the outcomes as well as the opportunity. You do not get to cast blame on anything or anyone else if you are not happy with the consequence.

If you cast blame or live as a victim, you have just given away the power in your ability to choose - you have given it to someone or something else. You are now powerless.

Free choice is also an issue at times because there can be too many possible choices, making it impossible to choose the best path. We can become paralyzed by a multiplicity of possible right decisions and end up not choosing at all.

Another area of problem is that once we make some choices, they are very hard to undo, you are stuck with the selection, and it may not be possible, without a lot of grief to undo that choice. Just try to undo a career choice, a marriage choice, having a child choice, purchasing a house choice, choosing to take an addictive substance, or getting into the driver's seat while intoxicated choice, and you will find out quickly that to undo these choices will be very costly. Attempting to undo destructive decisions is an attorney's bread and butter. You will want to avoid as many of these choices as possible. Life is hard; do not make choices in the direction of making it even harder.

Another issue with all these free choices is we do not live on a deserted island, our choices affect others, and their decisions affect us. Somehow, we need agreeable common ground, or else our options will end up causing a battle.

Another issue is that choices may also have significant limitations. There are some choices we do not get to make because of constraints in time, genetics, attributes, resources, legality, other obligations, and at times, just a limited number of choices.

Considering these problems, suddenly, this free choice does not seem free, and at times it is a significant burden. You have the privilege of free choice and the burden of being responsible for your choice. You do not get limitless "do-overs." If, however, you are wise, you do get to look at and evaluate the decisions made by others and their resultant consequences. In this context, we have a lot to learn from our parents; whether they were good or evil, they were examples of choices and outcomes we were able to closely observe.

Once we have accepted this burden for what it is and that it is present in every human, we can get to the point where it can be appreciated. When we get to the point of understanding the fact that we can choose our path but not our consequences, we are then free to dream and imagine within realistic parameters. The desired outcome should guide today's choices. We are now living life in the zone of the "if-then." If I dream of becoming a concert pianist, then I should get a piano, find a teacher, take lessons, and devote time to practice. If I desire to retire with an income for my retirement years, then I better start saving as early as possible. These are choices based on the desired consequence. It takes courage and perseverance to live deliberately, not caving to the urgent demands of the moment.

You are free to dream and imagine. Take time to ponder. About what are you passionate? What kind of person do you want to be? What kind of spouse do you want to become? What kind of parent do you want to be? What kind of grandparent do you want to be? Who do you want to serve? What legacy do you want to leave at the end of your life? Do not throw away your freedom for productive pondering. After all, it is your life, the only one you get, live it deliberately.

The burden of free choice and personal responsibility does not have to weaken you; it can make you stronger. How can this be possible? How can the burden of free choice and personal responsibility strengthen you? To be able to live with intent, to live more deliberately, is life changing. So, how can you do this?

First, it is essential to spend time in solitude for an honest appraisal. Take time daily to consider who you are and what you have. Embrace what you have as if what you have were seeds, seeds with incredible potential. Seeds you need to plant and maintain. In Psalm 5 verse 3 (TPT), the psalmist states: *"At each and every sunrise you will hear my voice as I prepare my sacrifice of prayer to you. Every morning I lay out the pieces of my life on the altar and wait for your fire to fall upon my heart."* Prayerful, meditative solitude will change your life. Take time, list your dreams, your gifts, your resources, and your options. What will you do with those seeds? You can choose to do nothing, you can throw them away, you can treat them carelessly, you can manage them casually, you can just put them aside, you can give them away, or you can plant them where they will grow and flourish. If you do this in the quiet of the day when there are no pressures for an action, you will find that you will become aware of many more options.

Secondly, take time to quiet the loud noise and demands of the urgent. You will always have urgent matters demanding attention right now, but most of those urgent matters are not necessary. Learn to separate the urgent from the important and at least spend some time considering the important - then you can move on to the pressing matters that demand attention.

Thirdly, write out your options. Be creative and list as many options as you can think of, even options you know you would never follow. Writing will help bring to the surface options you may have never thought of before, options that can provide a positive, creative solution to a stressful problem.

Fourthly, plan for essential choices and decisions. During your time of solitude, when you are pondering crucial life decisions like a spouse, education, work, hobbies, or housing, write a list of what is important to you. Feel free to dream; you have an imagination, use it. Try to make some of these decisions before they become a matter of urgency. The pressure of necessity will destroy your creativity and imagination.

Fifthly, take time daily for significant decisions. The decisions that determine what kind of person you will become because who you are is much more important than what you do. Be honest when you are evaluating your status, are you angry, are you bitter, are you greedy, are you self-centered, are you a victim, are you discouraged - be honest with where you are if you expect to get somewhere else.

Lastly, don't blame anyone else for your immediate consequences. If you blame you give away your power and the ability to make choices.

Being overburdened by free choice and personal responsibility will steal your ability to make decisions, kill your dreams and imagination, and destroy your ability to live deliberately.

Take time to pause and consider - it is your life - live it deliberately - it is your choice. God made you to be creative and productive as you walk with Him.

CHAPTER 9 - THE IMAGE – CREATIVE ABILITY AND POWER

With the first breath from God, a man received a portion of God's creativity and power. Humanity is not content being passive. Our God-given nature is to be creative as we interact with the rest of God's creation. We are to have a powerful impact, an impact in maintaining order in creation, benefiting one another, and bringing glory to God. We are to be active members of God's kingdom.

God is a God of creativity and unmeasurable power. God brought creation into existence with a spoken word. You see the evidence of God's creativity and power in what He has created. The works of His hands point to a compassionate, creative, all-powerful creator. *"In the beginning God (Elohim) created [by forming from nothing] the heavens and the earth."* Genesis 1:1

(AMP)

God gave humanity a creative role in creation. *"So, the Lord God formed out of the ground every animal of the field and every bird of the air and brought them to Adam to see what he would call them; and whatever the man called a living creature, that was its name."* Genesis 2:19 (AMP) We are to work alongside God and be co-creators. What a privilege and what a responsibility. God did the creating by forming the animals; Adam did the purposing by giving them their names.

Adam was then placed in God's garden to maintain order. *"So, the Lord God took the man [He had made] and settled him in the Garden of Eden to cultivate and keep it."* Genesis 2: 15 (AMP) The Hebrew word for "cultivate" means to serve through labor, and the word for "keep" means to preserve and to protect. We are stewards of God's creation and should not view ourselves as owners. We are protectors and not possessors. We are content in service and serving.

We were designed to use the creative power God has given us and to experience contentment in the provision of service. We were not made to be content with being served. God gave us His image, and that image is designed for action.

God gave humanity authority over creation. *"Then God said, "Let Us (Father, Son, Holy Spirit) make man in Our image, according* to Our likeness [not physical, but a spiritual personality and moral likeness]; and let them have complete authority over the fish of the sea, the birds of the air, the cattle, and over the entire earth, and over everything that creeps and crawls on the earth." Genesis 1:26 (AMP) To have dominion means to rule or subjugate. God continues to hold creation together, but humanity has a role in maintaining order and mastery. Fences still need to be built for provision and protection. While on a hunting trip with my father many years ago, we spent a night in the town of Maple Creek, Saskatchewan. It was Halloween, and some of the local young men thought it would be a great prank to open the gates at the local stockyard. Hundreds of cattle flooded onto the streets. It was chaos. The cattle trampled neatly trimmed lawns, broke fences, and left evidence of their presence on every road. It was a noisy, sleepless night. Within their corrals, they were safe, they had ample food and protection, but outside the corral was mayhem. It is much easier to maintain order than to try to regain order. Properly applied authority is an excellent thing.

Adam was placed in God's garden to cultivate. A man was made to work and maintain order. Living in this modern society of convenience, we have come to equate contentment with leisure. We couldn't be more wrong. Contentment is in service-focused work. We were not designed to "retire" in the sense of ceasing work. We are most content with a life of service. Yes, the form of service will change many times in one's lifetime, but if physically and mentally possible, we should always be engaged in service and order maintenance.

Adam was also placed in the garden to "keep" it. To "keep" the garden, Adam would have to value it; he would have to observe it and then work to preserve and protect it. Contentment comes with embracing the garden where God has placed you. Just like the forms of service that will change in your life, so will the gardens. Take time daily to thank the Lord for the gifts He has given, and for the garden where you are currently living. You have all you need this moment to live in supernatural contentment. Don't be like Adam and Eve, who thought they needed more to be more content.

For those first few days or years in the garden, Adam fulfilled his God-image of creativity and power by naming the animals, cultivating, and keeping the garden. With the arrival of Eve, things changed. *"Now the Lord God said, "It is not good (beneficial) for the man to be alone; I will make him a helper [one who balances him—a counterpart who is] suitable and complementary for him."* Genesis 2:18 (AMP)

Humanity's creative capacity and power were now to be used to be complementary to each other or to be helpful. The Hebrew word for complementary or helpmeet means, "a person that gives help, relief or aid." Our God-image was not designed to be content with self-service; we were made to complement one another. We were made to use our God-given creativity and power for the benefit of humanity.

What does it mean to have creative power? What is this creativity? What is this power? How do we use this creative power? What does it take to have creative power?

If creative power is to have a direction or focus, you need to be able to identify a need. The statement is true that; "necessity is the mother of invention." The more clearly you can define the need, the abler you will be to apply your creative power in the solving of the need.

As you identify needs and problems, embrace them, do not run from them. An unmet need should be a challenge and not an insurmountable problem. A need or problem seen as a challenge is kindling for your creativity. Value your God-given creativity; it has unbelievable potential and power.

With a need identified and embraced, now is the time to activate your ability to dream and imagine. Believe there is a creative solution. Desire to find the answer or solutions. Activate your God-given power-image to find the solution. If you are struggling, try to find what limits your imagination. We often limit our vision by our experience of past failures, fear, fear of future failure, consequences of action, or the negative voices of others. Take time to pause and give your imagination the freedom to explore options. Do not be limited by what others may think or speak. Thank God for your creativity and ability to dream and ask Him for guidance. You are only one creative solution away from a breakthrough.

It is essential to value the problem-solving process. If you want joy in your life daily, then appreciate the creative-power process more than the results. Results are episodic and, at times, maybe rare, but the process is a daily ongoing experience. Do not be pressured by the need for an outcome; it will only rob you of your joy and creativity. In Ecclesiastes 5:18 (AMP) it states; *"Behold, here is what I have seen to be good and fitting: to eat and drink, and to find enjoyment in all the labor in which he labors under the sun during the few days of his life which God gives him —for this is his [allotted] reward."* Your daily labor is your opportunity to activate your creative power, apply it with joy.

If you are free to enjoy the process, you are more likely to be patient. Take encouragement from Galatians 6:9 (AMP) *"Let us not grow weary or become discouraged in doing good, for at the proper time we will reap, if we do not give in."* Wait on God to give you solutions, Psalm 37:7-9 (AMP) *"Be still before the Lord; wait patiently for Him and entrust yourself to Him; Do not fret (whine, agonize) because of him who prospers in his way,"* Be patient, do not become discouraged by setbacks or the success of others. Be thankful and do not be pressured by the need for results. Enjoy every mile of the journey!

Do not take your creative power for granted or treat it lightly. As recorded in Ecclesiastes 9:10 (AMP), *"Whatever your hand finds to do, do it with all your might; for there is no activity or planning or knowledge or wisdom in Sheol (the nether world, the place of the dead) where you are going."* Whatever the task is before you, give it all you've got. And remember Galatians 6:9 (TPT) *"And don't allow yourselves to be weary or disheartened in planting good seeds, for the season of reaping the wonderful harvest you've planted is coming!"* Plant good seeds, enjoy planting good seeds, be persistent, and leave the rewards to God. If a coarse correction is needed, make the change, and keep moving. Hebrews 6:11 (TPT) *"But we long to see you passionately advance until the end, and you find your hope fulfilled."*

Adam's rebellion against God resulted in a fracture in the creative power component of man's God-image. Living with a fractured creative power-image is experienced as the burden of free choice and responsibility. God removed humanity from the garden. Creativity was now frustrated by necessity, fear, and disorder. Now to eat and exist required labor; not as much of life could be devoted to creative power or being creative, there were weeds to pick and thorns to remove. We were made to be creative and to exercise our creativity. We are content when we are using our creativity powerfully.

Apart from God, our authority role is warped. We now use our authority role over creation to have dominion over each other. Instead of using the power we have as an image-bearer, we turn our back to God and strive to gain control and power, relying on our own intelligence and strengths.

We no longer cultivate or labor to serve; we work to gain, focused on personal felt needs and desires. We may still work long and hard, but the purpose is misplaced and frustrated.

We abandon our role as keeper and protector, blinded by self-centeredness and oblivious to the consequences of our actions.

We have exchanged our role as complementing each other and building each other up for a self-centered life of self-protection and personal gain. I may appear to build you up, but I only do so if there is something in it for me.

With a fractured creative-power image, we focus on immediate needs like food, shelter, and comfort; we discard our creativity and power. We have become blind to the needs and problems requiring our God-given creativity and strength. We end up using a small fraction of our creativity and capability. We know we have potential, but our potential is frustrated and discouraged.

What we should see as a challenge we now see as a problem, and we avoid that problem. We lose sensitivity and insight into problem areas until they become a significant problem requiring an urgent response. In urgency, there is very little room for creativity or properly applied skills.

Exhaustion produced by the toil of life is death to the imagination. Dreaming and an active imagination is felt to be a luxury amid the disorder of daily life. We think we need to get things in order before we can dream or imagine.

The process of problem-solving has become tedious. If we determine our felt value in a result, we lose the joy of the process. At best, this gives us a life of short, episodic joy as we slowly burn out. We look at the results to determine the quality of our task or our worth as humans. In this process, we have made ourselves human doings. We sacrifice our God-image in exchange for a life of despair and desperation.

We now have pressure for measurable and predictable immediate results. Patience and pausing to dream and imagine are gone. The pace of life increases, and contentment fades away.

With no patience, there is no persistence. With a loss of stamina, there is a loss of commitment and a loss of passion. If we do not see immediate results, we give up before a breakthrough. We spend our lives wallowing in the muck of frustration and discontent.

The good news is there is healing for a fractured creative power-image. It is possible to regain a life of enthusiasm and strength. Colossians 1:21-22 (TPT) tells us about this restoration, *"Even though you were once distant from him, living in the shadows of your evil thoughts and actions, he reconnected you back to himself. He released his supernatural peace to you through the sacrifice of his own body as the sin-payment on your behalf so that you would dwell in his presence. And now there is nothing between you and Father God, for he sees you as holy, flawless, and restored,"*

Do not become discouraged when you feel weak and powerless. God has a plan for you, a plan to provide you with supernatural strength. As recorded in Ephesians 3:16 (AMP), *"And I pray that he would unveil within you the unlimited riches of his glory and favor until supernatural strength floods your innermost being with his divine might and explosive power."* With a fractured creative power image, you have not lost your creativity or your power. With God's help, your creativity and power that has been misplaced can be restored.

God's restoration plan for us, through Christ, provides healing for our fractured, frustrated creative power-image. We will still have weeds and thorns to deal with, but we no longer need to be tied up by a destructive, self-serving life purpose. We are now working, cultivating, serving, protecting, and inventing to establish His kingdom.

With a restored creative power-image, we no longer must rush around in a panic all the time looking for meaning and purpose in what we choose to do – we are free to pause. We can freely start our day with thanksgiving. We can give back to God all He has given us and work together with Him, where He would desire us to serve. We do not have to be pressured by the urgent demands of the day; we can pause and take time to consider the important. Lord, what would you have me do today? Lord, I pray that the scales of self-centeredness and self-service fall from my eyes. Lord, open my heart and mind to understand Your word. How may I be of service? Whom should I be serving today? Lord, what is my role in your kingdom today?

When our God-image is fractured, we are distracted. We are distracted by the burden and pain of isolation. We are distracted by the deep sense that what we do and who we are is meaningless. We are distracted by the weight and responsibility for the choices we make and the consequences we experience. With all this distraction, it is impossible to know and follow our God-given purpose. Our purpose today is the same as Adam's purpose at the time of creation. We are to cultivate and keep God's garden. God's garden is His kingdom. We are to be co-creators with God. We are to use our imagination, creativity, physical strength, energy, and power to serve God and His kingdom. We are not here or alive to build our personal empire. The possibilities are endless. We can draw, write, talk, work, build bridges or houses, create roads or paths in a way that demonstrates God's love towards us. As is says in Romans 8:28 (TPT), *"So we are convinced that every detail of our lives is continually woven together to fit into God's perfect plan of bringing good into our lives, for we are his lovers who have been called to fulfill his designed purpose."* We no longer must look for meaning and purpose from what we do; our meaning and purpose is in bringing glory to Him by laboring in His garden.

We are now free to use our creativity and power to serve God and our fellow man. Our security is in our relationship with God and not in our relationship with humanity. You are free to serve, even though your life will be a painful reminder to others that their God-image is fractured. Continue cultivating and keeping.

Living as God intended, we are also free to preserve. We are free from the pressure to possess or own for the sake of security. We are here to be stewards and not owners. If you see yourself as an owner, you live life desperately trying to hang on to what you have. You live with fear and pressure that you may lose what you feel you own. Your life becomes small, no larger than what you possess. When you live as a steward of God's provision, the pressure is gone. Loss in one area is an opportunity for God's provision in another. There is contentment for the steward that is not available to the owner. Live with open hands and a thankful heart.

Trust in the Lord frees you to create. So, dream, imagine, and move forward with thanksgiving. Hold on to the promise in Isaiah 40:31 (AMP). *"But those who wait for the Lord [who expect, look for, and hope in Him] Will gain new strength and renew their power; They will lift up their wings [and rise up close to God] like eagles [rising toward the sun]; They will run and not become weary, they will walk and not grow tired."* God will restore your creativity and power. If you live to serve Him and His kingdom, you will see awakened creativity and ability. This is the life of the restored God-image, a life of peace and hope as in Jeremiah 29:11 (AMP) *"For I know the plans and thoughts that I have for you,' says the Lord, 'plans for peace and well-being and not for disaster, to give you a future and a hope."*

How should we apply this God-given creative power? It is time to pause and take inventory of our life and the components of our life. We need to take inventory of all God has given us, our possessions, our time, our home, our relationships, our intellect, our history, our family, our passion, our everything and hand it all back and then be willing to wait. God's fire will fall.

With a renewed God-image, there is no reason to be controlled by fear. With a renewed mind and a restored imagination, we can now live as God intended. We can now dream and plan. We were designed to use our different intellectual abilities and interests in limitless creative ways. We often limit ourselves more by the fear of failure than by limited mental capacity. Lord, thank you for the mind you have given me. I give its capabilities back to you for your glory. Guide my dreams and imagination in directions that they may be used to build Your kingdom.

Our words have power. Our words can build someone up or tear someone down. Our words can be healing, or our words can cause pain. Our words can bring life, or our words can bring death. We need to give our mouth back to God. God has promised He will build us up; we do not need to rely on our words to promote ourselves. Words used for self-promotion only increase our distance from others. Words spoken to encourage or build someone up will build relational bridges. Lord, thank you for my ability to speak. Impress upon my heart when I should be silent and when I should talk. May my words be seasoned with grace and used for your glory.

An energized imagination will result in an action. These actions will take many different forms. Actions could look like researching a need, investigating options, building a prototype, diagraming a plan, or starting a business. One of the first points of resistance to any strategy is your most valuable resource, time. You can accomplish more with brief daily periods of action than waiting for a large block of time. Be patient and be persistent. A passionate, committed action plan is needed to bring any dream to reality. Do not forget; the joy should be in the process and not just in the results. Lord, thank you for the energy needed to bring about Your plans. Help me to be patient and passionate about Your kingdom. Guide the work of my hands.

Do not underestimate the power of your presence. Our presence should bring peace into a troubled world. If your goal in life is self-centered, your presence will betray you.

There is a lot of power in working together with others who have a common goal and mission. Working with others can bring clarity to a dream and vision. We benefit from the encouragement of others, and we benefit from encouraging others.

We are to be co-creators with God. We are God's representative,

His hands, and feet. Do not forget Matthew 5:13-16 (TPT) *"Your lives are like salt among the people. But if you, like salt, become bland, how can your 'saltiness' be restored? Flavorless salt is good for nothing and will be thrown out and trampled on by others. Your lives light up the world. Let others see your light from a distance, for how can you hide a city that stands on a hilltop? And who would light a lamp and then hide it in an obscure place? Instead, it's placed where everyone in the house can benefit from its light. So, don't hide your light! Let it shine brightly before others so that the commendable things you do will shine as light upon them, and then they will give their praise to your Father in heaven."* Your world needs your light. Live the image.

CHAPTER 10 - BURDEN OF MORTALITY

Psalm 103 verses 15 and 16 states (TPT): "Our days are so few, and our momentary beauty so swiftly fades away! Then all of a sudden, we're gone, like grass clippings blown away in a gust of wind, taken away to our appointment with death, leaving nothing to show that we were here." Life is short, and the longer you live, the more you realize how quickly time and life pass by. And then it is over. One day it will be over for every one of us; there is no escaping the reality of our mortality.

In this chapter, I will be dealing with the existential burden of mortality. Our eventual death is an issue faced by all human beings. For many, the subconscious anxiety caused by a fear of death is behind a lot of their daily anguish. This burden affects us all; we are all going to die. This fear of death or the fear of the process of dying is called thanatophobia. The essence of this burden is not death itself because it is unlikely, we can fear something we have not experienced. The nature of this burden is the fear of separation: separation from ourselves, others, our dreams, goals, what we value, our purpose, and our sense of meaning. What we fear is not death; we fear ultimate, permanent separation. We fear uncertainty and change, and death represents the most significant change we will ever experience, the shift from being to not being.

To honestly wrestle with this burden means we must struggle with our sense of meaning and purpose. As you approach the end of your life, you will face how meaningless and self-centered most of your life has been, and this can be a lot to bear. Having to face meaninglessness and life's disappointments will often lead to a crisis. The Hebrew word for hell is sheowl, meaning, a place of no return or a place of exile; this is the burden of mortality. We live in the shadow of hell. The fear of death is a reality we need to acknowledge and accept. It is not healthy to live oblivious to death or to live in constant fear of death. If we can gain an understanding of this burden, it will significantly aid in our ability to value and use the short time we are alive. Embracing the burden of mortality can substantially enhance your life.

So, in day-to-day living, how does this burden show itself? It may manifest itself as fear or anxiety. We will often disguise the fear of death with worry about our health or the health of those you love. This worry leads to a compulsive drive to get and stay healthy. In the medical field, we refer to these individuals as the "worried well." Billions of dollars a year are spent on supplements, health spas, and unproven innovative treatments, to push aside the concept of one's ultimate demise. Faced head-on, this burden of mortality is just too troubling, but the reality is we cannot deny our eventual death; it impacts our lives in many subtle ways. At times of separation or loss, the burden of mortality is more likely to show itself through activities, beliefs, or thoughts that are self-protective, self-absorbed, or self-nurturing. When we feel a threat, we do what we can to protect our fragile selves. These are times when one retreats from relationships or avoids intimacy. Intimacy in relationships requires us to be vulnerable, and when we feel threatened, we do not want to increase our felt vulnerability. This fear causes us to avoid solitude; solitude represents isolation, and isolation intensifies the awareness of loss. We experience increased discomfort in both intimacy and loneliness when we experience a significant loss, but there is some comfort in being part of an intimate group. Conformity brings a sense of safety. If the threat is long-lasting, this conformity can foster narrow-mindedness where there is adherence to a specific group with fear or avoidance of others who may think differently.

The experience of the burden of mortality varies from person to person. For the young, it is more likely to be experienced as separation anxiety where the elderly suffers the burden of mortality as angst about impending death. I have observed many very healthy individuals live in constant fear of death, and I have seen many people with a terminal diagnosis live in peace with a renewed freedom and compassion. It is almost as if those with a terminal diagnosis have the freedom to be and are no longer living under pressure to do.

This burden of mortality is a reality that affects all areas of our life. It is a reality too painful to address directly, so being the self-protective creatures we humans are, we have developed the fantastic skill of being able to deny what we do not want to face. Studies have shown most people do not believe they will die. Denial can be helpful as a way of finding a safe harbor while figuring out the next path to take, but if denial becomes a way of life, it quickly becomes destructive. When faced with the apparent reality of our death, it takes an enormous amount of energy to maintain a life of denial. We end up spending considerable amounts of emotional energy in the act of self-protecting. This type of denial is not deliberate deception or lying; it is psychological hiding from the truth or reality; it is honest self-deception. And humans are masters of this type of self-deception. We are in danger of spending so much energy on self-protection and denial we have no remaining power for other endeavors. We spend our valuable time self-protecting often unaware of what it is we are working so hard to protect.

What we are working hard to protect is a deep fear of exposure to realities too painful to handle. We try to deny we feel isolated and alone and try to hide the anguish of no sense of purpose or meaning. We work to protect ourselves from the shame and guilt of having chosen a life direction that did not go as planned, and the fear of ultimate separation. We are working as hard as we can to avoid an existential crisis about our meaning and purpose.

We end up wasting a lot of our life trying to fight or change what we cannot change. To accept the burden of mortality, we must address both the reality of our mortality and the denial that often accompanies that reality. The biggest problem with this burden is not accepting the fact that we will die someday. The biggest problem is permitting denial to control our life as we hide from what we are unwilling to accept. Accepting mortality is accepting reality – it happens to all of us – it is a reality we all must face. We all live with varying degrees of denial. We spend time and energy wrestling with mortality when we would be much better off spending our time dealing with the denial. Our mortality is a future reality; our denial is a present negative force. You need to accept your death to deal effectively with the denial.

The burden of mortality causes universal anxiety, and this anxiety is controlled with denial. A little denial for a brief period can be helpful; it can be a safe harbor during times of distress. The problem, however, is what serves as a fleeting comfort soon becomes a pattern of living, and the pattern soon becomes a lifestyle. We are now living in a dome of denial – not only regarding our mortality but regarding any area of our life that may cause emotional pain. We have become compulsive comfort seekers. If anything dares puncture our denial dome, we are quick to patch the hole with another dose of denial in the form of some self-destructive behavior like drugs, alcohol, excessive exercise, working long hours, embracing bitterness, or anger and on-and-on. We end up being hurt by our self-protective beliefs and actions, but our dome of denial must remain intact. Life is hard; it is hard for everyone; be very careful what you choose as your safe harbor.

Once we have accepted this burden for what it is and that it is present in every human, we can get to the point where it can be appreciated. Appreciating this burden involves acknowledging how much of our lives are consumed and therefore wasted by denial. If we accept our mortality, it will help lessen the power behind a lot of the denial in our lives. Less denial means a lot more energy for living.

So, what is the power and impact of denial? Denial does have the ability to protect, but this only lasts briefly. Denial can be powerful enough to distort reality and erase memories. Denial can prevent accurate evaluation and recollection. In this state, living in the dome of denial, other areas of life get confusing. Anything causing discomfort or pain, like relationships and responsibilities, increases our denial. This denial is the power behind the irrational thinking that is part of any addiction. Statements like, I don't know why I am gaining weight: I don't eat anything; this drug will not harm me, I am only hurting myself; drinking and driving is not a problem; this cigarette will not hurt me are all statements from the mind of someone living in the dome of denial. We end up living in a self-destructive world of myopic self-evaluation.

Denial may initially start as a self-protective defense mechanism to shelter us from the thoughts of early parental separation. As we age, denial has lots of opportunities to grow as we mature. Any significantly painful childhood event can substantially increase the growth and development of denial. The experience of abuse at a young age, the experience of trauma, or the death of a loved one can make life without denial seem impossible to bear. The main negative impact of adverse childhood experiences may be their effect on the development of denial. These are not the only things fostering more significant denial. Any event that alters your impression of reality can work to encourage the growth of denial. Growing up in affluence with the belief life should be smooth and pain-free will significantly impact your level of denial. This view of life is not reality; life is hard; it is hard for everyone, and no amount of money will change any of that. Life is not to be lived as a fantasy because the fantasy will only disappoint. Freedom in life comes with facing the painful and uncomfortable realities, recognizing all humans share these and that we can meet these realities with faith and perseverance. Facing life's difficulties and realities is hard and, at times, feels like it is too much to bear, but denying these realities will destroy you. Living in denial will produce momentary comfort, but long-term frustration and exhaustion.

The burden of mortality does not have to weaken you; it can make you stronger. How can this be possible? How can the burden of mortality strengthen you? Once we lessen the burden by seeing it for what it is, we are free to use this reality as a strength and not a burden. Remember, our battle is not with our mortality; it is with our denial.

To effectively deal with the burden of mortality, you must accept the reality that you are going to die. Your death, just like your birth, is a part of life: do not be afraid of it, do not ignore it, do not tempt it, and do not deny it. Don't waste your limited time on this earth, supporting denial and fighting a fight you will only lose. If you accept you are going to die, you will place a higher value on the time you are alive.

Learn to embrace your fears and your denial; by doing so, you will lessen their power.

Take active steps to limit your denial regarding your mortality. Calculate how many days you have lived and contrast this to how many days your parents and grandparents lived. It can be very sobering to realize you have an expiratory date: you will not live this side of heaven forever. Take time in solitude to ponder your life and not your problems. Your experience is unique; your issues are not. What kind of person are you, and what kind of person do you want to be? What do you want your legacy to be? Read obituaries and take some time to write your own. Do not shy away from the funerals of family or friends. Death is a reality.

Avoid denial by living authentically. Embrace times of solitude and be honest. You will hurt yourself and all those you contact if you live a lie.

Embrace a sense of wonder. A sense of wonder can help you get things into the right perspective. A sense of wonder can lessen the focus we continually have on ourselves and our problems. You do not want to get consumed by your emotional pain or the injustices you are facing. In Psalm 8:3-4 (TPT), we read, *"Look at the splendor of your skies, your creative genius glowing in the heavens. When I gaze at your moon and your stars, mounted like jewels in their settings, I know you are the fascinating artist who fashioned it all! But when I look up and see such wonder and workmanship above, I have to ask you this question: Compared to all this cosmic glory, why would you bother with puny, mortal man or be infatuated with Adam's sons?"* Wonder and awe put things into a proper perspective. The sense of wonder from gazing at the night sky, walking in the forest, or looking out over the ocean or the Grand Canyon will change you. Learn to embrace your puniness. A sense of wonder can slowly erode the cover on your dome of denial. You can learn to appreciate a sense of wonder in nature, works of mastery, music, or learning to see things from a different perspective. If you are not using up all your energy trying to prop up your denial, you can slow down enough to live your life and embrace the wonder all around you.

Be aware of what is really at the core of your fears and denial. Do not be afraid of the vulnerable part of you that is afraid of separation and isolation. Do not be controlled by the reality of your ultimate non-existence – your mortality. Do not miss the big picture by remaining self-centered and spiritually empty.

Be alert and on guard concerning denial. These are some of the signs that denial is active in your life. If you answer yes to any of these questions, denial is present. Have you lost your sense of wonder? Are you less compassionate and intimate with those you love or those who love you? Do you blame others for your present life situation? Are you living as a victim? Are fear and anxiety controlling you? Do you have an increase in irrational thoughts and beliefs? Do you demand and seek comfort at any cost? Does bitterness control you?

If you do not address the burden of mortality, it will feed your denial, steal your peace and clarity, kill your joy and compassion, and destroy your perception of reality. Do not be controlled by denial and the burden of mortality.

CHAPTER 11 - BURDEN OF SPIRITUAL EMPTINESS

I n the book of Psalms, chapter 6, verse 6 (TPT), we read: "I'm exhausted and worn out with my weeping. I endure weary, sleepless nights filled with moaning, soaking my pillow with my tears." Are you exhausted and worn out? Has your life turned out differently than you expected? Have you run out of answers? Do you feel isolated? Has life lost its meaning? Are you confused? The chances are if you think this way, you are spiritually empty.

In this chapter, I will be dealing with the burden of spiritual emptiness.

The first step in learning how to deal with this burden of spiritual emptiness is to acknowledge it exists and that it is a problem.

What is spirituality? What is spiritual emptiness? Why is spirituality important?

Spirituality is essentially restoration. It is the restoration of body, soul, and spirit. It is the path and process of reclaiming our relationship with God, learning to walk with Him, and not be in opposition to Him. It is the recovery of the image of God in man. It is the rebirth of our spirit with subsequent transformation in our soul and body.

Spiritual emptiness is the pursuit of comfort and a sense of completeness apart from a relationship with God. Man attempts to negotiate his life path, without depending on God.

We live in an age with lots of potential solutions to our problems that do not require reliance on God, so why do the spiritual things matter? We know about proper diet and exercise. We have beneficial models of psychology and philosophy. We have affluence and distractions that can keep us busy. We have never known so much about diet and exercise, yet we are more obese than ever. We have never had so much information on our psychology and emotions, yet the suicide and addiction rates are skyrocketing. We are rich in resources, yet poor in spirit. Something vital is still missing. We are all aware, deep inside us, there is someone, a master designer, who is much bigger than ourselves, and we were made to serve that someone and not to spend our life in endless self-service.

We are rarely aware of our spiritual emptiness. It is apparent when we are up against something much bigger than ourselves, like the threat of a significant loss or the struggle with an addiction. We are also aware of it during times of prosperity when, even if we have acquired everything we could want, we are still aware something vital is missing. This awareness is often written off as a bout of fatigue or emotional exhaustion when we are trying to fill our spirit with a substance that could never satisfy.

How do you know you are spiritually empty? What arc the signs and symptoms of spiritual emptiness? A spiritually empty life is a life of self-centeredness and self-promotion. All that matters are my experiences, my life, my comfort, and my image. I may be aware of others, but not aware of their pain or their struggle. The life mission of the spiritually empty is to avoid discomfort and pursue comfort, no matter what the cost.

If you are spiritually empty, you are proud; you think your way is the only way. You may be sweet and kind about it, but you are still arrogant.

If you are spiritually empty, you are also deceptive. You deceive others, and you deceive yourself. You work hard to hide your faults and point out the flaws in others - in an ever so lovely way.

If you are spiritually empty, you are not thankful or grateful.

You live your life with constant discontent. You are never satisfied.

These are several of the shreds of evidence of living a spiritually empty life, but the most significant proof is that you are living a life of constant comparison. You will find hallow contentment or increased discontentment in comparison with peers, your expectations, or with your former youthful self. We continuously use comparison as a tool to determine our value. From the time we are first born, the comparisons begin. We are weighed and measured and labeled based on our size. As life goes on, the comparisons continue.

Just pause for a moment to consider the many tools of comparison you experience on an average day. You have scales to weigh you, measuring tapes that size you, clothing sizes, IQ tests, school grades, credit scores, and of course, the big one, a mirror. We compare ourselves to others and our former selves, and in the end, we are not satisfied. If you score high on the comparison scale today, the result is pressure to maintain your position or arrogance because of your success. If you rate low on the scale, the result is discontentment. As you age, the person you see in the mirror every day becomes a fading vision of your once fit and fashionable self. Spiritual emptiness, the life of constant comparison, results in the life experience of quiet desperation, full of disappointment, and discouragement.

We end up wasting a lot of our life trying to fight or change what we cannot change. It is time to accept that, as people, we are all very self-centered. We grumble and complain that no one understands us. We believe no one can experience our physical or emotional pain the way we can, so we end up on a life-long personal mission to achieve comfort. When we are successful in gaining some degree of comfort, we become proud; when we fail, we become depressed and even more self-centered. To get what we feel we need, we become deceptive and, in the process, lose our authenticity. We are no longer thankful or grateful; we live discontented and dissatisfied in a sea of constant comparison. This experience is the living hell of spiritual emptiness, a life of quiet desperation where at best, we experience momentary comfort amid meaningless, endless distractions. It is a life of continuous self-service and fading compassion. All we care about is our comfort. We are willing to bend the rules because we see our circumstances as being unique, so society's rules don't need to apply to me. We live as bitter, lonely victims with no sense of meaning or purpose. Our thoughts and motives are awash with denial and irresponsibility. We are dependent on our environment to come through for us and lessen our discomfort. When our discomfort increases, we become more self-focused and more aware of our pitiful human predicament. We spend our life wallowing in discontent. Living this way is the definition of the burden of spiritual emptiness. We are all born with our backs turned away from God, determined to go our own way, and in the process of seeking comfort, manage to create even more discomfort and pain.

Once we have accepted this burden for what it is and that it is present in every human, we can get to the point where it can be appreciated. How can this burden be understood? If we recognized what the problem is and that it is an issue for all humans, we can stop comparing ourselves to one another and get on with addressing the real problem, our spiritual emptiness. If we are aware that where we are turning to address and fill our void will not work, then maybe we will have a chance to turn in a direction that will be productive. We do not have to remain spiritually empty. The problem, however, is it takes humility, honesty, courage, and gratitude to turn our lives around and seek God. It takes faith to believe there is a loving creator who has provided a way back to Him through the sacrifice of His Son. A sacrifice that meant He experienced all the physical pain, social isolation, and psychological anguish all humans have ever experienced. There is someone who knows what we are experiencing. He suffered it on the cross. He bore the weight of it for you. He has provided the path back to God. God has provided this gift, a gift we only need to accept.

The burden of spiritual emptiness does not have to weaken you; it can make you stronger. How can this be possible? How can the weight of spiritual emptiness strengthen you? So, what does spirituality mean? How do we become more spiritual? The answer is simple. In the book of Jeremiah, chapter 29 and verses 13-14 (MSG), *"When you come looking for me, you'll find me. Yes, when you get serious about finding me and want it more than anything else, I'll make sure you won't be disappointed."* The path to spirituality is the humble, courageous path of seeking God with your whole heart. As we take these steps, it is essential not to be confused by what spirituality is not. People and society promote many practices and beliefs as being spiritual that are nothing more than counterfeit spirituality.

Spirituality does not involve comparing yourself to anyone else. Spirituality is comparing yourself to what God has in store for you and living by His Word. Much of what we have equated with spirituality is nothing more than man's program to feel good about himself. I have worked with a lot of criminal patients over the years; as a group, most of them attend church regularly. They attend church, not for spiritual growth, but as a way of convincing themselves, they are good people, and how they conduct their life is not so bad. If you pause and look, you will find self-deceivers in every church. Are you one of those self-deceivers?

Spirituality is not the maintaining of a list of laws and rules. Laws, regulations, and boundaries are helpful to avoid negative consequences, but the keeping of commandments does not get you closer to God. A life focused on law-keeping will result in a lack of compassion and joy. Rule-keeping and law-focus is another mode of comparison we use to determine our value. If I keep more laws than you, then I am more spiritual than you – this is not spirituality; it is a force that drives people away from God and away from each other.

Spirituality is not a specific group of practices like meditation, prayer, or worship. Prayer, meditation, and worship are valuable elements of a relationship with God but are only weak psychological boosters outside of a relationship with God. Do not use these practices as a measure of your spirituality. Just because you pray longer than your spouse does not necessarily make you a more spiritual person than your spouse. Are you praying, meditating, and worshiping because of your relationship with God, or are you praying, meditating, and worshiping trying to gain favor with God?

Spirituality is not "sacrifice." A relationship with God should free us to be generous in our giving, but how much you give does not determine your level of spirituality. You should be free to give because of what God has given to you, giving out of gratitude and thanksgiving and not as a means of buying special fa-

vors from God.

Spirituality is not a specific diet or dietary code. You are responsible for what you put into your body. A specific diet will not get you closer to God. On the other hand, gluttony, alcohol abuse, and drug abuse are evidence you are spiritually empty. You are responsible for everything you eat, drink, smoke, or inject. Choosing to put anything into your body to alter your mood is evidence of spiritual emptiness.

Spirituality is not a belief. As it states in the Bible – "even the devil believes." It is more a matter of faith and seeking God than the knowledge of His existence. It is not just the belief; it is what you do with the belief. How have your beliefs changed your life?

Spirituality is not belonging to a specific group or club. Membership or attendance at a church or religious group does not make you spiritual. Encouraging one another of similar faith can be very uplifting and healing. It can promote a relationship with God, but it is not a relationship with God or a measure of your relationship with God.

Spirituality is not knowledge, wisdom, or reason. Spirituality is trusting God and not trusting your ability to reason. Those seen to possess knowledge, wisdom, or ability are tempted to rely on their strengths and not to trust God. Gaining knowledge and acquiring wisdom can help determine a path in life with more positive results than negative consequences, but exceptional mental skills do not equate with spirituality. Knowledge can help you see the wonder of God's creation. Wisdom can help you find a path with fewer negative consequences. Reason can help you evaluate your life, and if mixed with honesty, it can help you realize your knowledge and wisdom is not enough to build a relationship with God. A high intelligence quotient does not equal a high spiritual quotient. True spirituality is only a product of humble faith.

Spirituality is not doing something to gain God's approval; it is accepting what He has so graciously offered. Spirituality is not living with pressure to perform but living with thanksgiving for what He has provided. Try as hard as you like; it will not improve your walk with God. The effort and activities you use to gain spirituality may act as diversions, or a means to avoid painful areas in your life, but it will not bring you closer to God.

Spirituality is not just crying out to God for deliverance or personal comfort. Most people live their lives with no desire to relate to God. They carry on from day to day until some big disaster; then, they cry out to God to come through for them. God is gracious and, at times, will come through. Still, it is much better to develop this relationship before the going gets tough, at a time when the relationship with God may be able to guide you in a direction that could avoid some of those big disasters.

Spirituality is not a partial surrender or calling out to God to rescue in times of trouble. Spirituality is not surrendering in part or your life with the hope of seeing improvement, it is a surrender of all areas of your life. In my work in addiction medicine, I meet a lot of people who use surrender as a means of trying to build a stronger inner resolve to fight a craving. This type of surrender is more of a psychological trick to fight off an urge. Often the addiction wins this fight. Surrender and submission are all or none, and it is terrifying.

So, how would you rate your spirituality? Is spirituality important to you? Are you discontented? Are you spiritually empty? Are you working hard to achieve what God has given as a gift? Are you honest about your life? Are you humble? Are you grateful? Are you content? Where do you turn for answers to life's difficult questions? Do not forget the promise that if you seek Him, you will find Him - seek with your whole heart - God will not disappoint.

CHAPTER 12 - THE IMAGE – ETERNAL SPIRIT

I f you were born in Swaziland, you have a life expectancy of 32 years, but if you were fortunate enough to be born in Singapore, you have a life expectancy of 83 years. Life expectancy varies from country to country, but the angst caused by the burden of our mortality and spiritual emptiness is universal.

God is eternal. *"Do you not know? Have you not heard? The Lord is the everlasting God, the Creator of the ends of the earth. He will not grow tired or weary, and his understanding no one can fathom."* Isaiah 40:28 (NIV) God has been and forever will be, humanity, on the other hand, is confined by time. Our only experience involves time. We have a birth date; we have a death date; we are defined and restricted by time. It is almost too much for our little brains to grasp the concept of eternity.

The eternal God made man like Him, *"Then God said, "Let us make human beings in our image, to be like us. They will reign over the fish in the sea, the birds in the sky, the livestock, all the wild animals on the earth, and the small animals that scurry along the ground."* Genesis 1:26 (NLT) The spirit that God gave us with His breath is eternal. We have an immortal spirit.

A component of the image of God is the possession of an eternal spirit.

When we pause to ponder the days of our lives and all we have experienced, we know that God made us for more than much of what we have experienced. *"He has made everything beautiful and appropriate in its time. He has also planted eternity [a sense of divine purpose] in the human heart [a mysterious longing which nothing under the sun can satisfy, except God]—yet man cannot find out (comprehend, grasp) what God has done (His overall plan) from the beginning to the end."* Ecclesiastes 3:11 (AMP) A significant part of human experience is the angst produced by this longing in our soul.

So, what is this eternity God has planted in our hearts? What does it mean to have a spirit? What is this God-given eternal spirit that is part of the God-image? In John 4:24 (AMP), we read, *"God is spirit [the Source of life, yet invisible to mankind], and those who worship Him must worship in spirit and truth."* God gave us an eternal spirit with His life-giving breath, a spirit designed to worship Him with all we say or do; 1 Corinthians 10:31 (AMPC)

"So then, whether you eat or drink, or whatever you may do, do all for the honor and glory of God." If we lack contentment in our lives, it is because we are not doing what we should do to bring glory and honor to God. Discontentment occurs when we attempt to live to bring glory and honor to ourselves. As recorded in Micah 6:8 (MSG), we do not have to make life very complicated *"But he's already made it plain how to live, what to do, what God is looking for in men and women. It's quite simple: Do what is fair and just to your neighbor, be compassionate and loyal in your love, and don't take yourself too seriously - take God seriously."* We were made to have eternal priorities and values. What are your priorities, and what do you value? Considering eternity, how do your preferences line up? Several years ago, I asked a close friend how he was able to remain so calm in the middle of a stressful situation. He answered that he would evaluate the situation and pause to consider the impact the situation would have six months in the future. So, even though his present situation seemed urgent and demanded action, he was able to remain calm because the impact of the present problem would have very little meaning in six months. We should be living with an eternity mindset when it comes to our priorities.

When I first started a medical practice in northern Saskatchewan, Canada, in 1981, I purchased a "fixer-upper" cabin on a beautiful lake. I felt I had paid too much, so I spent every spare weekend working hard to increase the cabin's value. We spent our family vacations working on that cabin, and I began to feel that the cabin owned me. After three years of work, we stalked the cabin for the winter and returned home. Less than a month later, that cabin burned to the ground — all our hard labor up in smoke in one night. Yes, there were valuable times during that renovation project, it was great to work with my two young sons, and we did take some time to enjoy God's beautiful creation, but for the most part, my efforts to improve the cabin amounted to a small pile of ash. Most of what we do will end up the same way. We need to pause and consider eternity. What will be here ten thousand years from now? Our expensive homes, cars, toys, money, and jobs will be a small pile of ash. What will remain will be our spirit, the spirits of other people (even the ones that have hurt us), and the spirit of God. Where does that reality fit into your life priorities? Do you value the soul of your enemy more than the paint on your car? Lord, help us to pause and realign our priorities to be in line with Your preferences! Help us to bring glory and honor to You in everything we say or do!

We are designed to have a sensitive spiritual awareness. As written in Romans 8:16 (AMP), *"The Spirit Himself testifies and confirms together with our spirit [assuring us] that we [believers] are children of God."* We are made to be sensitive and aware of God's whispers. The world around us and the world within us is bois-terous with a noise that often drowns the whisper of God. If you are not hearing God's still small voice, it is not that God has to speak louder. It is a matter of silencing the other loud voices of pride, self-centeredness, fear, and pretense – with this quieter, you will find your hearing is just fine and God's voice is loud enough.

A life filled with lies, deception, and pretense is an empty, ex-hausting life. We can live freely, openly, and transparently with a restored God-image. It takes a lot of effort to maintain a lie. As described in John 3:19-21 (MSG), we should be walking in God-light; *"This is the crisis we're in: God-light streamed into the world, but men and women everywhere ran for the darkness. They went for the darkness because they were not interested in pleasing God. Everyone who makes a practice of doing evil, addicted to denial and illusion, hates God-light and won't come near it, fearing a painful ex-posure. But anyone working and living in truth and reality welcomes God-light so the work can be seen for the God-work it is."* Don't waste your life and energy living a lie.

Our awakened eternal spirit should generate within us ongoing gratitude. As described in Hebrews 12:28 (AMP), *"Therefore, since we receive a kingdom which cannot be shaken, let us show gratitude, and offer to God pleasing service and acceptable worship with reverence and awe;"* Our restored God-image should be a life seasoned with gratitude, worship, praise, and grace. Our spirit has been reborn. For this, we should be thankful.

Our sense of security comes from what we trust. Misplaced trust or broken trust causes fear and insecurity. Our eternal spirit was made to trust fully in God. As stated in Isaiah 26:3-4 (AMP), *"You will keep in perfect and constant peace the one whose mind is steadfast [that is, committed and focused on You—in both inclination and character], Because he trusts and takes refuge in You [with hope and confident expectation]."* While in medical practice in northern California, my boys and I took up the hobby of rock climbing. Now, I do not like heights. To this day, I get queasy looking over a dam or off the side of a bridge. The rock climbing required countless hours of practice, learning knots, testing anchor placement, and proper care of the equipment. With this practice came trust, trust in the process, and trust in the equipment. With this trust, combined with a purpose (climb the rock wall) and a focus (where is the next hand or foothold?) there was no fear. Should we not trust in the Lord more than a manmade rope? Should we not be able to live life without being controlled by anxiety? Jeremiah 17:7-8 (AMP) *"Blessed [with spiritual security] is the man who believes and trusts in and relies on the Lord And whose hope and confident expectation is the Lord. For he will be [nourished] like a tree planted by the waters, that spreads out its roots by the river; and will not fear the heat when it comes; but its leaves will be green and moist. And it will not be anxious and concerned in a year of drought nor stop bearing fruit."*

We have an eternal spirit that will exist forever. John 3:16 (AMP) *"For God so [greatly] loved and dearly prized the world, that He [even] gave His [One and] only begotten Son, so that whoever believes and trusts in Him [as Savior] shall not perish, but have eternal life."* We are living in a part of our eternity right now. How does this reality affect your life? Are you living today as if your brief life on earth is a dress rehearsal for heaven? We should be practicing and living praise and thanksgiving, not bitterness and frustration. For what kind of heaven are you rehearsing?

When humanity rebelled against God, our eternal spirit was fractured. A fractured eternal spirit is at war with God's Holy Spirit. We experience the anguish of a broken eternal spirit as the burden of mortality and the weight of spiritual emptiness. Galatians 5:16-18 (TPT), *"As you yield freely and fully to the dynamic life and power of the Holy Spirit, you will abandon the cravings of your self-life. For your self-life craves the things that offend the Holy Spirit and hinder him from living free within you! And the Holy Spirit's intense cravings hinder your old self - life from dominating you! So then, the two incompatible and conflicting forces within you are your self-life of the flesh and the new creation life of the Spirit. But when you are brought into the full freedom of the Spirit of grace, you will no longer be living under the domination of the law but soaring above it!"* When our eternal spirit is fractured, we focus on the physical more than the spiritual. The essence of what we can see, feel, taste, hear, and smell becomes more important than the spirit. We no longer pause to consider the wonder of the creator. We sacrifice the wonder of our spiritual being as we strive to satisfy our physical senses.

Another impact of living with a fractured God-image is that we focus on the temporal and neglect the eternal. We strive to get the most out of today with no acknowledgment of eternity. We define as necessary what is immediate and urgent. We need to learn to number our days as we consider eternity. Psalm 90:12 (AMP) *"So teach us to number our days, that we may cultivate and bring to You a heart of wisdom."* You are not living in preparation for eternity; you are living the "this side of heaven" eternity today.

The restored God-image is the antidote for the burden of mortality and the weight of spiritual emptiness. Life with a fractured image awakens fear of loss, fear of separation, and fear of ultimate demise. This fear is a powerful force, too powerful to live with, so we live our lives in denial as we try to hide from our debilitating fear.

Denial is the source of all sorts of damaging irrational beliefs that we cling to for comfort. In my work with patients who are addicted, these irrational beliefs are often fatal. We play with fire, believing we will not get burned. What irrational beliefs are you holding on to for comfort?

Living with fear and denial forces us to be focused on the immediate. Thinking about the future is too painful and generates too much fear, so we become preoccupied with our present felt needs and desires. If we focus intently on today, we do not have to think about eternity.

This fractured God-image life is self-absorbed and self-protective. If God is not my rock, then I must be my rock. If God is not who I trust, then I must trust myself. If God does not take care of me, then I must do all I can to take care of me. If there is no relationship with God, there is only me; I make myself my god. It is no wonder we struggle with our purpose and meaning. Our life and priorities are contrary to our design when we are living in fear, denial, and self-worship. We are no longer living as God created us to live. We are out of sync with our creator and with our God-image. We are self-absorbed and cling to our irrational beliefs, and we wonder why we are not content.

We do not have to keep living contrary to the God-image. God has provided a way to healing and restoration. *"Even though you were once distant from him, living in the shadows of your evil thoughts and actions, he reconnected you back to himself. He released his supernatural peace to you through the sacrifice of his own body as the sin-payment on your behalf so that you would dwell in his presence. And now there is nothing between you and Father God, for he sees you as holy, flawless, and restored,"* Colossians 1:21-22 (TPT). We no longer need to be weighed down by the burden of mortality or the weight of spiritual emptiness. Our fractured God-image can be reborn.

God has promised that if we seek Him, we will find Him. Matthew 6:33 (AMP), *"But first and most importantly seek (aim at, strive after) His kingdom and His righteousness [His way of doing and being right—the attitude and character of God], and all these things will be given to you also."* When we are not under the control of fear or denial, we are free to reevaluate our priorities and values. Values and priorities in keeping with a restored God-image bring peace and contentment. We no longer must waste our energy and life in endless self-service or self-protection.

Increased spiritual awareness can free us from being self-centered, arrogant, deceptive, ungrateful, and living with our worth based on comparison with others. Romans 8:6-8 (MSG) *"Those who think they can do it on their own end up obsessed with measuring their own moral muscle but never get around to exercising it in real life. Those who trust God's action in them find that God's Spirit is in them—living and breathing God! Obsession with self in these matters is a dead end; attention to God leads us out into the open, into a spacious, free life. Focusing on the self is the opposite of focusing on God. Anyone completely absorbed in self, ignores God, ends up thinking more about self than God. That person ignores who God is and what he is doing. And God isn't pleased at being ignored."* To live with a restored spirit is life and peace.

God knows all; God sees all. With a renewed God-image, we can live transparently. Hebrews 4:13 (AMP), *"And not a creature exists that is concealed from His sight, but all things are open and exposed, and revealed to the eyes of Him with whom we have to give account."* It takes a lot of energy and effort to maintain a lie. Yes, to live transparently will hurt, and at times, you will be mocked for it, but the alternative of living a self-protective life will destroy you. If you want to be whole and free, live transparently. James 5:16 (AMP) *"Therefore, confess your sins to one another [your false steps, your offenses], and pray for one another, that you may be healed and restored. The heartfelt and persistent prayer of a righteous man (believer) can accomplish much [when put into action and made effective by God—it is dynamic and can have tremendous power]."* Do not imprison your spirit and minimize your life by living a lie.

A restored spirit is a grateful spirit. Hebrews 12:28 (AMP), *"Therefore, since we receive a kingdom which cannot be shaken, let us show gratitude, and offer to God pleasing service and acceptable worship with reverence and awe;"* Being thankful today will prepare you for heaven. Take time to express your thankfulness to God daily. If you feel weighed down by the issues of your life or the problems of the world, write a gratitude list.

A life with a renewed God-image will have properly placed trust. Proverbs 3:5-6 (AMP) *"Trust in and rely confidently on the Lord with all your heart and do not rely on your own insight or understanding. In all your ways know and acknowledge and recognize Him, and He will make your paths straight and smooth [removing obstacles that block your way]."* Strive to be trustworthy and seek out others who can be trusted, but do not forget Psalm 118:8 (AMP), *"It is better to take refuge in the Lord than to trust in man."*

Live in the light of eternity. Pause and consider what has eternal value and what does not. Apply yourself wholeheartedly to everything you do. Do not be self-absorbed. Consider others and their turmoil. Live the image.

CHAPTER 13 - LIVING IN A WORLD OF FRAC-
TURED IMAGE-BEARERS

The first man was created complete and placed in God's perfectly designed world. God created man to experience fulfillment in a quality relationship with Him, aware of his value and purpose, active and creative with power, with an eternal spirit. We were made to be both physically alive and spiritually alive. God created humanity with all that was needed to be completely content. With disobedience came a fracture in our God-image. Now there was a problem. We still have God's image, but its expression and experience have become severely distorted.

God is patient, God is kind, and God has provided, through His Son, a path of restoration. God loves you and is wanting to relate to a humble, honest, and thankful humanity. Psalm 139: 5-6 (TPT) is an expression of this kind of love. *"You've gone into my future to prepare the way, and in kindness, you follow behind me to spare me from the harm of my past. With your hand of love upon my life, you impart a blessing to me. This is just too wonderful, deep, and incomprehensible! Your understanding of me brings me wonder and strength."*

We do not need to fear the future; God has gone into our future to prepare our way. Even when things seem dark and uncertain, God has prepared our future. You do not need to be anxious about tomorrow or paralyzed because of your past. We do not have to be controlled by guilt, shame, offenses, past abuse, or injustices. We do not have to live a life of misery and bitterness. There is hope. Because of a loving God, we can be free from anxiety about the future and harm from the past and live with thanksgiving today. Relationship with God is the only effective treatment for life's misery.

"Then God said, "Let us make human beings in our image, to be like us. They will reign over the fish in the sea, the birds in the sky, the livestock, all the wild animals on the earth, and the small animals that scurry along the ground." Genesis 1:26 (NLT) God imprinted humanity with His image. If we live consistent with the image, we are content, but if we live contrary to the image, the consequences are emptiness, greed, bitterness, discontent, pain, and turmoil. This fractured image is why we all struggle with the burdens that are common to all humanity. We all, to

some degree, struggle with the same things. Life is hard. On the surface, it may seem some struggle more than others, but we are all tempted to turn our backs on God to the same degree.

In God's grand creation, humans are unique. We all bear His image. We are not the same as other mammals. We have the image of God and an eternal spirit.

As an image-bearer, no matter how hard we try to deny God, we know there is a God, a benevolent, intelligent creator and that we are not that creator. *"For ever since the creation of the world His invisible attributes, His eternal power, and divine nature, have been clearly seen, being understood through His workmanship [all His creation, the wonderful things that He has made], so that they [who fail to believe and trust in Him] are without excuse and without defense."* Romans 1:20 (AMP) We do not have to feel pressured to convince people there is a God. The knowledge of God is already in them and is evident everywhere you look in God's creation. There is an intelligent creator, a loving, intelligent creator.

Unfortunately, the knowledge there is a God does not mean we seek Him. On the contrary, we all try to hide from God. We all have our ways to protect ourselves from God. We hide from God through open rebellion, denial, drugs, or alcohol. We can also hide in innocent appearing ways like computer games, work, service, and on and on. We are skilled at running and hiding. We justify the hiding by focusing on the injustices we have had to endure. We feel we deserve to be bitter. Bitter towards our fellow man and resentful towards God.

We are all greedy and self-serving. Our only experience of this world is through our own eyes, and we become blind to the life and struggles of others. We are here for ourselves. Apart from a relationship with God, we all, whether sweet or nasty, follow a self-serving life path. If we are not God-serving, we are self-serving. What has been self-serving soon becomes self-consuming. All the self-serving acts we have performed, and all the self-serving stuff we have gathered will eventually burn.

Discontentment is a part of every human's life experience. The result of being a fractured image-bearer is discontent. This discontentment is often deep and painful. The pain of this discontent causes us to be self-focused and self-protective. If you drop a concrete block on your foot, you are not likely, at that moment, to be thinking about your neighbor's struggle with life. We become fixated on our pain. When you focus on pain, it only makes that pain more intense.

As fractured image-bearers, we are all equally tempted to turn from God and seek our way. We try to make our life work and lessen the pain of discontent. The light from God's presence reveals our deception and self-centeredness, and this exposure is painful, so we run and hide.

All humans struggle with the burdens of isolation, meaning-lessness, free choice and responsibility, mortality, and spiritual emptiness. All our significant struggles involve one or more of these areas. These are the categories of temptations and struggles that cause us to turn our backs on God. The pain of these struggles compels us to look for solutions that are within our power and control. We do everything in our ability not to become dependent on God and, in the process, become dependent on our irrational beliefs and schemes.

We know there is more because God has planted eternity in our hearts. This life on earth cannot be all there is. We do all we can to quiet this unsettling feeling. We use distraction, denial, activities, and possessions to gain some sense of superficial peace. None of our ingenious schemes work, so we end up living in quiet discontent or open misery.

Discontent becomes discomfort, which then drives our actions and motives to seek comfort. Comfort at any cost becomes life's main priority. Compulsive comfort-seeking quickly turns into an addiction.

As a fractured image-bearer, if we happen to cross paths with a restored image-bearer who is content, we feel threatened. Their contentment uncovers the reality that all our self-centered efforts have not worked. We do not want our secret comfort plan exposed, so we avoid those who have a restored God-image and huddle together with fellow fractured image-bearers.

Living the life that God intended – the life of a restored image-bearer brings contentment. The life of the fractured image-bearer is a life of discontentment and frustration. The fractured relationship-image is experienced as the burden of isolation. The fractured substantial value-image is experienced as the burden of meaninglessness. The fractured creative power-image is experienced as the burden of free choice and responsibility. The fractured eternal spirit-image is experienced as the burden of mortality and the burden of spiritual emptiness.

Thankfully, God has a plan for restoration – a way for us to regain the restored God-image. *"Even though you were once distant from him, living in the shadows of your evil thoughts and actions, he reconnected you back to himself. He released his supernatural peace to you through the sacrifice of his own body as the sin-payment on your behalf so that you would dwell in his presence. And now there is nothing between you and Father God, for he sees you as holy, flawless, and restored,"* Colossians 1:21-22 (TPT) We can live the image as initially intended and do not have to remain in a life of misery.

A person with a restored image that lives to bring glory to God is an insult to Satan and will, therefore, come under attack. The attack comes from three primary sources; our unrestored mind and emotions, threatened fractured image-bearers, and the culture of antichrist.

Our spirit has been renewed, and we can live as God intended, but we still have an unrestored mind, habits, emotions, and desires. We need to present our bodies as a living sacrifice, and our minds need ongoing renewal. Romans 12:1-2 (AMP), *"Therefore I urge you, brothers and sisters, by the mercies of God, to present your bodies [dedicating all of yourselves, set apart] as a living sacrifice, holy and well-pleasing to God, which is your rational (logical, intelligent) act of worship. And do not be conformed to this world [any longer with its superficial values and customs], but be transformed and progressively changed [as you mature spiritually] by the renewing of your mind [focusing on godly values and ethical attitudes], so that you may prove [for yourselves] what the will of God is, that which is good and acceptable and perfect [in His plan and purpose for you]."* Our minds are renewed or washed by God's word. Ephesians 5:26 (TPT), *"to make us holy and pure, cleansing us through the showering of the pure water of the Word of God."* We are now on the path from misery to peace. The process is one of humbly coming before the Lord, asking Him to search our hearts and identify and root out the irrational thoughts, the untamed emotions, the damaging habits, and the ungodly desires. We can rest confident in Philippians 1:6 (AMP), *"I am convinced and confident of this very thing, that He who has begun a good work in you will [continue to] perfect and complete it until the day of Christ Jesus [the time of His return]."* If you are drowning in misery, take time daily to ask God to search your heart and then have the courage and faith to change what He reveals to you. At the end of your day, as you prepare for bed, pray Psalms 139:23-24 (TPT), *"God, I invite your searching gaze into my heart. Examine me through and through; find out everything that may be hidden within me. Put me to the test and sift through all my anxious cares. See if there is any path of pain I'm walking on, and lead me back to your glorious, everlasting ways - the path that brings me back to you."* If you abandon this growth process, it will not take long, and you will find you will again be struggling with the burdens of a fractured God-image.

If you follow this path, do not expect appreciation from your previous group of family and friends. If you have been part of a group that shares their bitterness and you move in a godly path, you will face rejection from your former bitter friends. Your contentment is a threat to their beliefs, irrational thinking, and their way of life. You bring with you God's light, and this is a threat to those hiding in the darkness. They hide knowing they are not living as one should; they know their deeds are self-centered and evil. They don't want your light around. If you become offended because your previous social group rejects

RICHARD ARTHUR HINDMARSH MD

you, you may resort to your previously destructive irrational thoughts as a way of escape. You can expect every area of the previously mentioned burdens will be under attack. The attacks can leave you feeling more isolated. They can cause you to question your purpose and meaning. They will challenge your dreams and abilities. The turmoil caused by these attacks can be noisy enough to impact your ability to hear God's still small voice. Stand firm, God is faithful, even when your family and friends are not.

You can expect another attack on your restored God-image to come from the culture of antichrist. So, what is the culture or spirit of antichrist? How do we identify it? God, the Father, through Jesus Christ, has promised to meet your deepest needs. He has provided a way for the restoration of your God-image. He has promised you peace and security in Him. Any culture or system that offers these promises in the absence of Christ is the culture of antichrist. 1 John 4:2-3 (TPT) informs us of the test we can use to identify the spirit of antichrist. *"Here's the test for those with the genuine Spirit of God: they will confess Jesus as the Christ who has come in the flesh. Everyone who does not acknowledge that Jesus is from God has the spirit of antichrist, which you heard was coming and is already active in the world."* The spirit of antichrist is the proclamation of God's promises without Christ. The spirit of antichrist masquerades as "the truth" when it is a lie. The spirit and culture of antichrist promise compassion but then cause division by elevating one group over another. Groups based on gender, ethnicity, sexual orientation, or financial status have special treatment. On the surface, it appears to be loving, but it is only causing more profound division. The culture of antichrist promotes the belief that what I can make of myself is more important than how God made me. It supports the wrong notion that I can find peace by changing who I was made to be. The culture of antichrist glories in deception – lies for the sake of lying. It promotes a life of hiding and a life of secrets. Bonds develop with those with whom you share secrets, not relationships based on God's truth. With the culture of antichrist, there is a loss of the sacredness of life. The economy and convenience are more important than human life, especially the life of the most vulnerable – the unborn. The culture of antichrist is a twisted road; it looks like it is going one way when it is going another. The culture of antichrist may also show itself as being perverse through open rebellion and open denial of God's existence. The culture of antichrist promises protection as it promotes fear; the greater the fear, the greater the need for the protection promised. The culture of antichrist fosters dependency. If I can simultaneously increase your fear of heart disease and then guarantee solutions to that medical problem, then you are now dependent on me. I have become your savior. We live in an age where the culture of antichrist is flourishing. Be wise; do not get swayed by the subtle culture of antichrist.

We are to live the image. It is a privilege to live the image. How do we do this? How do we live the image in a world of fractured image-bearers? How do we thrive and grow in godliness in a crooked and perverse world? What is the meaning of Philippians 2:12 when it states, *"continue to work out your salvation [that is, cultivate it, bring it to full effect, actively pursue spiritual maturity] with awe-inspired fear and trembling [using serious caution and critical self-evaluation to avoid anything that might offend God or discredit the name of Christ]?"* This renewed God-image life is only possible if we follow Paul's advice in Philippians 2:5-9 (AMP). *"Have this same attitude in yourselves which was in Christ Jesus [look to Him as your example in selfless humility], who, although He existed in the form and unchanging essence of God [as One with Him, possessing the fullness of all the divine attributes— the entire nature of deity], did not regard equality with God a thing to be grasped or asserted [as if He did not already possess it, or was afraid of losing it]; but emptied Himself [without renouncing or diminishing His deity, but only temporarily giving up the outward expression of divine equality and His rightful dignity] by assuming the form of a bond-servant, and being made in the likeness of men [He became completely human but was without sin, being fully God and fully man]. After He was found in [terms of His] outward appearance as a man [for a divinely-appointed time], He humbled Himself [still further] by becoming obedient [to the Father] to the point of death, even death on a cross."* If we expect to thrive and grow, we must humble ourselves as Christ humbled Himself. We need, with the help and comfort of the Holy Spirit, to live without regard to our reputation. We must lay aside our self-centeredness and pride and seek Him.

The individual with the restored God-image will pursue the most important relationships in their lives. The most important relationship is the relationship with God. Take time to talk to God, ask Him questions, look for answers to your questions in His word. Secondly, value your relationships with other people. Follow the instructions given in Philippians 2:4 (NKJV) and *"Do not merely look out for your own personal interests, but also for the interests of others."* Do not just rapidly pray for others; take time to consider their "personal interests." Ask yourself, what is it like to be (_____)? (fill in the name of the individuals you will meet today). If you find your love for others has grown cold, you will find it starts to warm again if you take the time to consider their "personal interests." To help with this a little more, I would like to introduce a concept called "burden filtering." Your love grows cold because you have become preoccupied with the miseries of your own life.

The pain of the burdens results in self-focus, and this causes our love for others to grow cold rapidly. Following the advice in Philippians 2:4, will begin to warm your compassion. Take five minutes daily for the next seven days and consider someone else. Now "burden filtering" is not just thinking about them; it is filtering your thoughts about them through the burdens described in the previous chapters. Make a list of the people you are going to consider. The list should include a parent, your spouse, or a close friend, someone much younger than you like your child or grandchild, a person of prominence you admire, a homeless person that stands on the street corner with their cardboard sign, and a friend. You should also include someone you dislike, like someone who has mocked you or caused an offense. Now take five minutes to consider that person in the light of the burdens. Do they struggle with a sense of isolation and meaninglessness? Are they struggling with their decisions and purpose? Are they struggling with their mortality, and are they spiritually whole? Are they struggling with issues of trust? Are they aware that God loves them? Do not use this time to compare their struggles to yours. Assume that their battles are currently more intense and painful than yours. Remember, we are to consider others above ourselves and not less than ourselves. Once you have completed this time of "burden filtering," it is time to pray.

Start by thanking the Lord for them, thanking Him that He loves them more than you ever could, thank Him that John 3:16 applies to them as much as it does to you. Ask that the word of God's love come to them and offer yourself to deliver the message of hope. Ask the Lord to prepare your words and provide the opportunity. Ask that the Lord send other believers across their path, someone who they will listen to that can guide them to Him. Ask that the scales of doubt, denial, self-centeredness, and spiritual blindness fall from their spiritual eyes. Ask that the Lord protect them so they may feel the consequences of their life direction but not suffer harm in pursuing that direction. If this "burden filtering," followed by prayer, becomes a regular part of your life, you will find you start to see others as God sees them, and your compassion will warm. Boundaries will still be necessary, but at least you will be able to set them with kindness.

By seeking God to address your emptiness and setting aside greed and bitterness, you are now free to live your life as originally intended. With a restored God-image, you are free from having to determine your value in your heritage, accomplishments, wealth, position, associations, or property. What you depend on for your sense of value owns you. God Himself owns you now; He paid the price for your freedom. You are now free from the exhausting efforts you used to spend to gain a sense of

value apart from God. You can now live with realistic expectations and priorities that will bring contentment and fulfillment. This freedom will unleash your creative power and bring
life and substance to your dreams and imaginations, so you can
find and fulfill your role in making the world and God's kingdom
a better place.

With a restored God-image, you no longer must live being
controlled by fear. We can live with the promise in Romans
8:31(AMP) *"What then shall we say to all these things? If God is for
us, who can be [successful] against us?"* We no longer feel the need
to waste our life hiding, guarding secrets, or living in denial.
God is big enough to handle any reality. We are free to be humble and honest.

A restored God-image means we are more spiritually intact and
aware. We understand the meaning of Ephesians 6:12 (AMP),
*"For our struggle is not against flesh and blood [contending only
with physical opponents], but against the rulers, against the powers,
against the world forces of this [present] darkness, against the spiritual forces of wickedness in the heavenly (supernatural) places."*
We are aware that there is a lot more going on than we see on the
surface.

How are we to live the restored image in a world of fractured
image-bearers?

In the ideal situation, in a world of restored image-bearers, relationships would be straight forward; people would love one another; they would be trustworthy and authentic. We will have to wait for that world. So, how can we live the restored relational image amongst those who feel the pain of separation and isolation?

We should have the attitude of Philippians 2:5 (AMP) as a guide to relationships this side of heaven, *"Do nothing from selfishness or empty conceit [through factional motives, or strife], but with [an attitude of] humility [being neither arrogant nor self-righteous], regard others as more important than yourselves."* This attitude will impact the quality of our relationships, give love a definition, help with proper placement of trust, and encourage authenticity. The Bible tells us that they will know we are Christians by our love and that we are to love others as we would love ourselves. Love, compassionate consideration of others must be balanced this side of heaven with boundaries. My work with people suffering from addiction is an excellent example of the importance of this principle. If I provide compassionate care without limitations, it will be interpreted as a license to continue a self-destructive lifestyle. These boundaries can and do save lives. Take time to think of appropriate boundaries. Boundaries are necessary for all our human relationships. At times these boundaries must be written out and signed, especially if you are in the awkward position of raising a rebellious teen. Be courageous enough to state the boundaries. Consider what should be appropriate boundaries.

Our relationships should be compassionate and loving, but problems arise when we talk about trust. It is relatively easy to love, it is challenging to trust, yet it is the level of trust that more clearly defines the quality of a relationship. Trust should be based on someone's actions and not just their words. Some of the hardest criminals will speak some of the sweetest, kindest words. Trust is essential, but it must be with caution. Be patient in your judgment. The Bible tells us it is by their fruit we will know someone. Develop your skills as a fruit inspector. You need to maintain clear boundaries while you wait to see the fruit of their life. Be honest and trustworthy but be wise when it comes to trusting others. You do not want to permit ongoing injustice and offense.

Strive to be authentic. Be honest and humble. Cherish your solitude time with God, ask Him daily to search your heart then be willing to change what needs to be changed. The more authentic you are, the more clearly you will recognize authenticity or the lack of authenticity in others.

In an ideal world, we would all work together, and our meaning and value would be secure in who we are in a relationship with God. We would all cooperate and work to elevate one another. There would be no competition or striving for meaning, value, or purpose; we would have a clear understanding of our God-provided value.

Living with a restored God-image means you are fully aware of your God-given substantial value. This awareness should produce an attitude of thanksgiving. Whether you succeed or fail in a task, your value as God's child is secure. Your life should reflect the words of the psalmist in Psalm 107:1 (AMP), *"O give thanks to the Lord, for He is good; for His compassion and loving-kindness endure forever!"* Are you this thankful? Are you full of gratitude for all that God has done for you? If this thanksgiving is waning, then it may be time to ask why.

It may be time for a humble and honest evaluation of where you draw your sense of meaning and worth. Pause, look at all you have or all you desire, and give it all back to God and let Him energize you.

2 Chronicles 7:14 (ASV), *"if my people, who are called by my name, shall humble themselves, and pray, and seek my face, and turn from their wicked ways; then will I hear from heaven, and will forgive their sin, and will heal their land."* Humble yourself and pray, God will lift you, and He will restore your thanksgiving as you find your value in Him.

As a restored image-bearer whose value is secure, you are now free to serve others. 1 Peter 4:10 (AMP), *"Just as each one of you has received a special gift [a spiritual talent, an ability graciously given by God], employ it in serving one another as [is appropriate for] good stewards of God's multi-faceted grace [faithfully using the diverse, varied gifts and abilities granted to Christians by God's un-merited favor].*" Your value does not come from your gifts or talents; they were given to you by God; you do not own them; you are a steward. Use what He has given you, whether that is much or little to serve others.

We are to be co-creators with God and other image-bearers. With a restored God-image, we have the freedom to approach a task as God intended. We can rely on our God-given creativity and curiosity to pursue our dreams with passion and commitment.

We are free to use our God-given talents and abilities to dream and imagine solutions, businesses, inventions, and so on to serve God and others. Acts 2:17 (AMP), *"And it shall be in the last days,' says God, 'That I will pour out My Spirit upon all mankind; And your sons and your daughters shall prophesy, And your young men shall see [divinely prompted] visions, And your old men shall dream [divinely prompted] dreams;"* It is time for God's people to wake up and dream!

You are free to use your energy to focus on a task and not be distracted, trying to gain a sense of meaning or attempting to avoid the consequences of destructive decisions. You can push ahead with diligence. Colossians 3:23-24 (AMP), *"Whatever you do [whatever your task may be], work from the soul [that is, put in your very best effort], as [something done] for the Lord and not for men, knowing [with all certainty] that it is from the Lord [not from men] that you will receive the inheritance which is your [greatest] reward. It is the Lord Christ whom you [actually] serve."* If you are serving yourself, your diligence will dissolve, and you will become discouraged. Do all you do as if you are serving the Lord.

You can now live your birthed dream with passion and commitment with the energy to see the vision come to reality.

You no longer must live being controlled by fear. You are secure in your relationship to God and no longer need to be controlled by fear of failure or reliance on an excellent result to be confident in yourself. Isaiah 41:10 (AMP), *"Do not fear [anything], for I am with you; Do not be afraid, for I am your God. I will strengthen you, be assured I will help you; I will certainly take hold of you with My righteous right hand [a hand of justice, of power, of victory, of salvation]."*

With a restored spirit, we can now live with the right priorities. We no longer need to live in denial because of fear produced by our sense of mortality. We can begin to see and prioritize as God sees and prioritizes. We can understand what will last and what will burn.

The restored God-image is aware of the need to continue to renew your mind and present yourself as a living sacrifice. We see the tension between the flesh and the spirit and the need for intervention and help from the Holy Spirit. Romans 8:6 (AMP), *"Now the mind of the flesh is death [both now and forever—because it pursues sin]; but the mind of the Spirit is life and peace [the spiritual well-being that comes from walking with God—both now and forever];"*

We should be living with eternity in mind and living to build and support God's kingdom, not striving to create our own little empire. Is eternity in your mind?

We should value what has eternal value. Pause to consider what will last and what will not last. Where is your focus? What do you value? What do you treasure? Luke 12:34 (AMP), *"For where your treasure is, there your heart will be also."* If your heart is troubled, it is because you have rotting treasure. Live today with eternal priorities and values.

You are unique. God loves you. You can have a meaningful relationship with God. As His child, you have substantial value. You have God-given creative power. God gave you an eternal spirit. So, go out and live the image as God intended, free from loneliness, meaninglessness, the pressure to perform, and anxiety about your mortality.

"The Lord bless you, and keep you [protect you, sustain you, and guard you]; The Lord make His face shine upon you [with favor], And be gracious to you [surrounding you with lovingkindness]; The Lord lift up His countenance (face) upon you [with divine approval], And give you peace [a tranquil heart and life]." Numbers 6:24-26 (AMP)

Live the image as God intended.

ABOUT THE AUTHOR

Richard A. Hindmarsh

Dr. Hindmarsh holds a bachelor of arts in sociology from the University of Saskatchewan and a master of arts in counseling from Grace Theological Seminary. He is a graduate of the University of Saskatchewan Medical School. He lives with his wife in Lebanon, Oregon, where he is currently the medical director of Samaritan Treatment and Recovery Services.

Web page: fracturedresilience.com

PodCast: Fractured Resilience

Email: fracturedresilience@gmail.com

BOOKS BY THIS AUTHOR

Now I've Gotcha!

Addictive chemicals from sugar to meth

Fodder For Ponder

Embracing boredom to enrich your life.

Stress Undressed

The five primary causes of stress.

Deadly Roots

The subtle destructive power of bitterness.

Manufactured by Amazon.ca
Bolton, ON

14912328R00106